where the t...

things are:

feathered essays

WHERE THE TINY THINGS ARE: FEATHERED ESSAYS

Nicole Walker

First published in 2017 by Peanut Books
A literary imprint of punctum books, Earth, Milky Way
www.punctumbooks.com

ISBN-13: 978-1-947447-22-6 (print)
ISBN-13: 978-1-947447-23-3 (ePDF)

LCCN: 2017954625
Library of Congress Cataloging Data is available from the Library of Congress

Cover image: RS52013 Electron microscope image of penguin feather
Photographer Gerry Nash, © Australian Antarctic Division

Book & cover design: Valerie Vogrin

Contents

Microscopium

In the 1968 film, *The Powers of Ten*, Charles and Ray Eames adjust the lenses of their cameras and zoom out. It begins with a 1-meter-square of an image of a man at a picnic in a Chicago park, viewed from 1 meter away. Every 10 seconds the lens moves 10 times farther away and the field of view grows 10 times larger. Cars. Docks. 1,000 meters. City on the lake shore. Edge of Lake Michigan. Then the whole lake. 10 to the 6th—earth as solid sphere. Then, whole earth. Good night moon. Paths of planets: Venus, Mars, then Mercury.

Then, that sun, casts its imposing light all over. But then everything disappears. Oh universe. How did you grow so small?

On Sunday night, a former student, Jordan, age 21, was riding her bicycle through a neighborhood south of the school when another 21-year-old, drunk, drove her F-150 66 miles per hour through that neighborhood. A neighborhood is only as big as the streets are wide, as the reflectors are bright, as the sidewalks are thick, as the stop signs are red. This was a small neighborhood. So small that a driver, driving fast, can't even see it. The driver, driving fast, drunk, exponentially, shifts into the ten to the seventh power and there, there is no bicycle. There, there is no girl with hair as black as the paint on your truck, as black as your skid marks as black as the sky beyond the reach of the sun.

That is the problem with death. In the zooming of both time and space, you become smaller and smaller. Now, you're a picture on the cover of the *Arizona Daily Sun*, a newspaper so small the crease is a cut, and thereby you are halved again.

And then we pause and start back home. This emptiness is normal. The richness of our own neighborhood is unique. Let's go home. 2 seconds per exponent this time. 10 to the 7th, 6th, 5, 4, 3, 2, 1. Let's reduce. Let's go smaller. 10 to the -2, approach the surface of the man on the picnic, cross layers of the skin, tiny blood vessels, an outer layer of cells, a capillary containing red blood cells, then into the nucleus of the man's cells, holding the heredity of the man, the coiled DNA itself, in an alphabet of 4 letters, the code for the man, 4 electrons. Quantum motion. At 10 to the minus ten we enter a vast inner space. The carbon nucleus. So large and so small. The domain of universal modules. A single proton fills our screen, fuels our scene.

Jordan is still full of potential energy. Jordan's carbon atom still dots the curb. Those protons still shimmer with the quantum energy. If only we could get to know Jordan again, at this quantum level. A class held on the side of the road, her words as inky as 10 to the 40th power, her words as resonant as the hydrogen bonds that keep the street, the grass, the tire, the bumper, the metal, the thump, the braking, braking, braking all together.

◎

Micromeat

If you're going to eat meat, you should buy the meat locally. If you're going to eat meat, you should make sure the animal didn't suffer in a small box or a large box or shit in a lagoon or spend its life trampling over streams, destroying salmon spawning grounds, or being shipped from one side of the country in a boxcar with open-air panels or shipped back in a refrigerated semi-truck. If you're going to eat meat, you shouldn't shove the meat full of antibiotics so that you're conspiring to help the superbugs become resistant to antibiotics. You shouldn't hobble the animal as it's put on the conveyer belt toward the ends of its life. You shouldn't daze the animal with drugs or stun guns before you slit its throat.

If you're going to eat meat, you should buy the meat locally. So local that it might mean homegrown. So local that you raised four goats in the backyard and let the goats have sex and get pregnant and have tiny goat babies that you fed from a bottle. But, if you're going to eat meat that local, you shouldn't count the babies. You shouldn't name the babies. You shouldn't or maybe you should, introduce your children to the goats. You shouldn't, or maybe you should, let your children watch as you whet the knife against the stone you couldn't find locally so you bought through Amazon.com.

You should invite your friends over, especially the ones with whom you read *The Iliad* at Reed College. You should remember how hungry that book made you. A roasted goat. The beginning of Western Civilization. You should make an offering to your household gods. You should try to think of this as an offering—to the CAFO cows, to the sweet neighbors who don't complain about the smell, to the truck drivers who didn't have to drive this goat to you, to the mother of this goat and the mother of your child, to your child that you couldn't decide whether or not to let watch and so you do because knives are decisive and goats are small but this one has big eyes into which you are trying not to look, into which you are trying to erase as you've erased so many cows' eyes in the past. You don't look at your daughter's eyes either. You look at the fur on the throat. You try to think of it as a wool blanket. You've seen wool blankets spun before your eyes before. You can part that weave. You should be able to part this one. For the first time, you know the pleasure of pre-wrapped meat. You would give anything for the protective film of plastic right now. A little black foam. Oh steak. Oh Safeway, you think as you do something you have no training for, as your friends, those who read *The Iliad,* turn away and only your wife holds the feet and only you drag the blade across the throat and only you turn the baby goat upside down to let the blood drain out like you read you were supposed to on Wikipedia.

You build a fire. You dig a pit. You bury the dead baby goat. You layer oregano and lemons on top. Sprinkle salt. You put coals on top of the meat and let it roast like any good Achaean. The smell of smoking meat brings the friends back. It brings the neighbors over. Someone said they could smell the smoke all the way down the street at Reed College. The goat, cooked, is unlike anything you've ever tasted. The goat is all the meat you've ever wanted.

The next year, when the baby goats are born, you dig into your pockets, find a twenty-dollar bill, and take it to Safeway to celebrate new life.

◎

Microbarriers

Inside the human organism live up to five thousand species of microorganisms. Different strains of each species multiply. A human, standing on a scale, weighs as much in micro as she does in macro, if you count the weight of the dust mite and the weight of the digestive enzyme. But these gut microorganisms represent the diversity and colonizing power of the human-bacteria relationship. The small intestine, unrolled and split open like an earthworm under the microscope, spans the area of a flayed blue whale—the largest organism on the planet. Inside the flayed whale they would find as many species of microorganisms in the whale's intestine as inside the human's. Flayed, both whale and human intestine span an area large enough to park seven school buses. Inside the seven school buses are 47 children, each with his or her own histrionic number of microorganisms, which, in the mind of a first grader, look like little earthworms. If you want to get someone to eat an earthworm, try first graders, who will eat anything baked in brown sugar that reminds them of a gummy worm. Earthworms carry their own microorganisms like Dionysus carried his bota bag filled with wine, but gummy bears not so much. You can tell a baked-in-brown-sugar earthworm from a gummy worm by the way, when you flay them, a million microorganisms spill out.

Where the human starts and the world begins is determined inside the gut. The microorganisms perform a border. Although they are the world inside you, they also protect you from the world, and, truly, from themselves. The gut microbes make a barrier between you and the outside world, although they, outers, are also inners. They are a paradox, these microbes. The microorganism can try to kill you if his name is *Clostridium botulinum,* but your friend, *bifidobacterium*, can keep him from completing his mission. *Lactobacillus* fights *E Coli* every day. Imagine a million Greek soldiers in the horse that is your gut. You are together in this fight, *Bifido* and horse, whale and *lactobacillus.*

When the world was not of you, you were not of this world. Not until you journeyed through your mother's birth canal did the previously non-organismed inside of your body become colonized with bacteria. The vaginal canal and its microorganisms infected you. And now you are safely infected with the world. Inside out, you thank the barrier for keeping in check the salmonella. You thank the bacteria for possibly holding back the proliferation of viruses, microorganisms even smaller than bacteria that are just using you like the bad boyfriend you had in ninth grade for your willingness to replicate and host another species in your body. At least bacteria have mutual respect for one another. Viruses bring nothing to the table. They don't even open the car door for you. They just line the passenger seat with condoms they pretend to wear.

The gut barrier, like a good condom, keeps bad bacteria out. The good bacteria neutralize the bad if they get in. I read today about a shooting inside the parliament building in Canada, a two-year-old dying from the Ebola virus outside a hospital, a soldier joining the Kurdish Army inside Iraq, a Voter ID law approved in Texas, a shelf sloughing ice into a cold but warming sea, a deer, foot caught in a fence, dying trying to get it out. I do not want these words inside me, but my ears do not serve as a barrier device. My eyes do not act as a barrier device. My forehead does not act as a barrier device. My skull does not act as a barrier device. My brain, perhaps if had been raised on yogurt's probiotic features, could act as a barrier device, but alas, alack, this brain has no way to keep the outside out.

◎

Microsurgery

They still use a saw to cut off a leg. It's circular now in the twenty-first century but the chiseling teeth are still a quarter of an inch long and curved as a scythe. I imagine something so much softer, a pink eraser from grade school that just gently removes, rolling pencil lead off paper cleanly, if not wholly.

One of the first bad scenes in a movie I saw—I'd like to think it was Oscar-winning *Das Boot* auf Deutsch but was probably just the Sunday night movie I was allowed to stay up for a cringe—a man lay in the bottom of a life boat and his companions handed him a knife to bite down on as they cleanly and wholly removed his leg.

When my sister found out they had to remove my grandmother's gangrenous leg, she said, "Don't worry grandma, I'll get you a bullet to bite on." And "Well, now you won't have to dress up for Pirate's Day anymore." I wished I could have said something funny instead of crying and making pointless circle motions with my hands.

How old do you have to be for the vascular surgeons to give up? At eighty-five, their microtools lay on the bottom of a lifeboat, unmovable for all the waves of diabetes and knots of veins. At sixty-five, they might take the microscope to a vein, see how much shaking hand the cell walls could tolerate. At fifty, they'd go in. You have good proteins, good platelets, and a steady line of health insurance. At forty, they're banging to get in there now—hello, I'm a pirate. I've come to practice on your relatively soft and pliable capillaries with my microhook and microsails.

But at eighty-five, my grandmother lies in her hospital bed with a foot as rotten as any German film. Her leg does not pulse like it did in elementary school, or in high school, or when she got married the third or the fourth time, or when she gave birth to my mother, sixty miles from home in the town of Coalville where they let her stay in bed for a week. She luxuriated in every moment of that hospital stay—the one during which her daughter came early but breathed on her own, where her nurses wouldn't let her get out of bed, instead brought her every meal—one, two, three, sometimes even four a day, the one hospital she knew she would walk out of.

◎

Microencephaly

When Zoe was almost two her pediatrician made her have an MRI to see what kind of encephaly was happening inside her head. How much foot down can you put when the doctor measures her head circumference to be a 110 percent of normal? Can you say "I know she's fine" because you know she's fine without sounding like you doth protest too much? What if you're wrong (even though you know you're not) and her brain pushes against the already-large circumference of a skull like a flooding river against a high-built dam? So you give in and let them lay her down on the table. You let them put the cotton balls on her eyes. You let them fire up the magnets and let rays happen against her head like the sun happens against the planet and look what you get? An image of the world all inside her head. Birds sheltering squirrels hiding under owls inside trees cutting out canoes on top of fjords shadowing granite slab and then flower burst after flower burst inside of which of course seed then lettuce then tomato a whole salad for a brain. The world is best protected nestled inside itself like matryoshka dolls and her head is big, yes, but also large and expansive, and if there's anyone I would entrust, and I mean "en" to read "in," it is my large-headed daughter who woke up from the anesthesia and wanted to get the hell out of there.

My son and husband and daughter each host huge heads. They make fun of me for my smaller-sized head which I say is not that small, and I tease back saying I hope you don't tip over, top-heavy, planet-sized-head-riddled babies. I put hat upon hat upon them and they never do fit.

◎

Microlecithal

She was a student in Nancy's class, not mine. I only saw her because she was visiting the writing center and I was working at the writing center although I don't write there all that much. She was wearing not quite a burka but her head was swaddled and her dress was a robe, trailing on the floor. In the desert, the robe makes some sense—it keeps the sun from burning skin. The long hem of the skirt skims sand, rushes air up, underneath. On that side of the world pointing fat side to the sun, long and covered yet light and breezy makes sense. The headscarf translates to Flagstaff weather. In the winter, you want to keep your head covered, especially in the morning when the temperature blips between plus one and minus one, plus one and minus one. But those skirts drag in the snow. The edges soak. Melted snow inches up the robe. All day long, you become wet in a way you fear might offend Mohammed.

She hadn't felt the baby kick for three days. She is eight months pregnant on the other side of the world from home and she does not know what this means. This is her first baby. She came here because the Center for International Education invited her husband, and her husband invited her. She is a student of English and yet the word "kick" doesn't translate here. She wonders if it's the cold that's slowing the baby down. She wonders if it is the thin air here. She wonders if it is the way the earth contracts away from the sun, this far north, at this elevation, like a Gap girl tightening the belt on her low-cut jeans. Nancy asks me if it is normal for babies to be so quiet for three days. I say, sometimes, when it's warm, the baby doesn't move. But I don't know what I'm talking about. When I was pregnant I was cold all the time and the baby came early—before the eight months pregnant she is.

Later that day, she sent Nancy an email. She had gone to the health center as Nancy had suggested. At the health center, in a language she was studying but couldn't quite say was her own, she heard the nurse practitioner tell her that the baby had died. Inside her, as she had walked through snow, the baby was already sloughing off cells. The baby was already decomposing under that veil of dress and skin. Under that skin, the baby that had made the skirts billow forth, the stomach that had made its own equator, collapsed and contracted. The baby that she was supposed to be holding up fell down. She couldn't tell her husband, any more than she could tell her mother, that it was the baby who had kept her gravitationally erect. Now, baby-shrinking, head collapsing, skin-sloughing, her skirts weighed more than the sun itself. The equator shrank. She slips across the now-flat of the world as if upon ice.

◎

Micropreemies

It's the not knowing that's the worst. In *What to Expect When You're Expecting*, they tell you what to look for: cramping, fluid, blood. But they don't tell you much after that. Even though your doctor prescribed a Unisom-equivalent to help you sleep and to keep the nausea down, you woke up to eat a banana every morning at 2 a.m. But at least you kept the banana down, which is more than you could for the first twelve weeks of your pregnancy.

When, almost five months pregnant, you felt the first wave across your stomach, you thought it was plain morning sickness. Morning sickness and waves went together. The first trimester, you felt like you'd been on a boat. Your body rocked with the growing fetus—moody upswings and downswings, up all night, asleep all day, food went down, food came back up. You thought "rocking" but perhaps "wracking" was more appropriate. Still, you'd wanted this. You and your husband had been trying to get pregnant for three years. You had, until you started trying to get pregnant, thought yourself a regular woman. Three years of intrauterine insemination (IUIs), the drug Clomid to increase progesterone, and injected hormones to stimulate regular woman hormones in your own body made you think about your hormones differently. Made you think about "regular" differently. Now you wondered whose life you had been living—you had always pictured yourself with a baby, one in your arms, on your shoulder, against your hip, hugging your leg. Instead, you have other people's and other animal's hormones coursing through your veins. How much "not you" would have to go into making your baby? You'd discussed in vitro fertilization. Even donor eggs, with the obligatory injections of progesterone and other hormones you were not, as yet, required to know the names of. If you could erase that medical jargon from your mind, you would. You won't even explain the words.

It is Michigan in winter, 2004. Streetlights turn on at four in the afternoon. Through their sodium glare, you look out into the street. You eat rice while looking out the window through the lights. You eat crackers at ten. The lights glare orange. At two in the morning, banana in hand, the lights seemed dimmer. Is the sun coming up already? It's too early. You count how many nights you'll be up like this—staving off nausea. Eating tiny meals. Not sleeping as a talisman against bad things happening, as if consciousness could affect the development of fetal brain tissue. Butter does help brain tissue, you know. You should stay up to eat more butter, but butter makes you feel sick, so you hope the fat in crackers makes up for it. You expect crackers to pull double-duty. Make baby brains and keep you from throwing up.

But you don't exactly feel like throwing up. The tightening you feel goes all the way across your stomach, around your back, and up through the umbilical cord, like you're pulling a belt too tight. The belt tightens, then it loosens. Maybe this is the quickening, one of those magic words that does not make you think of medicine but instead of something natural and outdoorsy. You think that roots of trees might quicken with that first sip of rainwater after a long drought. Strawberries quicken when the ephemeral blossom turns to solid fruit. The shaking of a Northern Flicker's egg. You're trying to listen to your body, like the midwife you would have used would have advised. But because of your advanced maternal age, thirty-five, you were considered too high-risk and assigned to Dr. Florens, who you like but don't love. He uses words like hypertension and gestational diabetes rather than quickening. It doesn't matter, now, it seems. Doctor vs. midwife, it doesn't matter: at this point you can't listen to your body because your body is making these moves noiselessly. You can't figure out what's going on because the waves keep coming, and you are only twenty-three weeks and four days pregnant, and the only thing this could be you are almost certain it can't be.

But it is.

Causes: A micropreemie is a baby born weighing less than one pound, twelve ounces (800 grams), or before twenty-six weeks gestation. Because they are born months before their due dates, micropreemies face long neonatal intensive care unit (NICU) stays. Although many extremely premature babies grow up with no long-term effects of prematurity, others face severe health problems throughout life.

Micropreemies are very fragile, and every day that a pregnant woman stays pregnant increases her baby's chance of survival. About ten percent of babies survive at twenty-two weeks. At twenty-four weeks, sixty-six to eighty percent. After twenty-six weeks, ninety percent of babies survive.

Yearly, thirteen million babies are born prematurely across the globe—over one million of them die from preterm birth. The number of babies being born early grows every year. The number in the United States has grown thirty-six percent in the last twenty-five years. How could this number increase when healthcare is supposedly getting better? Pregnant women have better access to prenatal health care than ever. Humans supposedly know more than they did. How can we be going backward?

One theory is that for every "advance" humans make, there is an equal step back. For instance, the consequence of making it possible for previously infertile people to become pregnant may contribute to preterm birth, especially if the mother has more than one fetus implanted via in vitro fertilization (IVF). In developed countries, high blood pressure, being overweight, and delaying pregnancy contribute to preterm birth. In developing countries, a lack of nutrition contributes to preterm birth. Tobacco, drug, and alcohol use also unite—all three contribute to mothers giving birth too early across the globe.

It's not just a mother's intrauterine environment that causes preterm delivery. The larger environment may play a part. According to a 2009 health report from Environmental Health News, University of California researchers found higher instances of preterm babies born in Long Beach/Orange County. The researchers compared women who lived in Los Angeles neighborhoods with the most traffic-related pollution to women who lived in the neighborhoods with the least traffic pollution. Reviewing the birth records of more than 81,000 infants, researchers found that those in the polluted areas were 128 percent more likely to deliver "very preterm" babies. Fetuses are vulnerable to the toxic substances inhaled by their mothers, theorizes Jun Wu, an assistant professor of epidemiology at UC Irvine and the study's lead author.

Babies born prematurely can suffer long-lived consequences. For example, prematurity is one of the primary risk factors for developing cerebral palsy. It's generally agreed that the earlier in the pregnancy that the baby is born, the greater the chance that the child will have impaired cognitive skills or behavioral disorders, as well as chronic problems with vision and hearing.

Science keeps finding ways to keep smaller and smaller babies alive. The risk of poor outcomes doesn't offset a doctor's ability to sustain that just-born baby. Technologies adapt to make survival in an artificial environment possible. As scientists begin to discover the causes of premature birth, the understanding of "environment" becomes complicated. As the neonatologists and surgeons with microscalpels practice their skills on these micropatients, as they adapt their machines and their tools to suit these ever-newer patients, the micropreemies themselves have shown an ability to adapt. The babies' bodies adjust to artificial lights to remove the bilirubin from their livers. Their skin learns to absorb warmth from heated incubators, and to metabolize intravenous fluids, where originally they metabolized food through the placenta via the umbilical cord.

Even the mother's body can react to change. Micro-premature infants have different metabolisms and dietary needs than infants born at term, and mothers who deliver infants prematurely supply milk that is higher in protein and fat.

Micropreemies have critical periods of time for growth and development. There is new, key knowledge in these critical periods that we can and have learned from the preterm infant. By paying attention to these tiny creatures, scientists may also discover insight into medical conditions across populations. An article in *Newsweek* explains new research on how the placenta communicates important information to the fetus. The placenta has been, up until recently, a mostly ignored organ, but in trying to explain why premature births are happening more often, researchers began to study the neglected placenta. They found that the placenta sends developmental signals to the fetus in the form of chemicals, hormones, and gases. Sometimes, these signals won't be read by the body for years. Cutting off this communication early may mean that the body never receives certain signals. "Without the placental signposts, development is hobbled," Anna Penn, a neonatologist at Packard Children's Hospital in California says. "If we can figure out exactly what directions have been lost, we can chart an identical map and help keep development on course." Two things they discovered: both progesterone, which helps nerve cells to grow, and oxytocin, which protects fetal neurons from becoming over-excited and dying, appear to reach peak concentrations late in pregnancy. In young children, low concentrations of the hormone have been linked to social and behavioral difficulties. The study of preterm placentas and premature babies who become autistic children may provide insight into the causes of autism in all autistic children.

You have never really thought about the way fish breathe before. You, computerless, (and even if computered, there's no Wi-Fi in this wing) cannot Google "fish respiration." You don't know exactly how that baby is breathing inside you. Fetuses don't have gills, as far as you know. The red blood cells in the baby's veins are oxygenated with your breath, through the placenta that you imagine looks like a very large bag of haggis.

You wonder about the many ways you're sure this is your fault. You picked up that heavy living room chair to vacuum underneath the other day. You drove in the car over that bumpy road. You had sex, ate spicy food, slept on your stomach, walked three miles, slipped on the snow, ate pickles, ice cream, the pastry that compensated for the glasses of wine you weren't drinking. You had an actual glass of wine. You ate garlic. You took a bath. You took a shower. You parted your hair on the left. It was all your fault, and now, suddenly, or perhaps just noticeably now, your baby, who is not able to breathe except in a very fishy way, dependent on magic and miracle to pull oxygen from the water, is going to be introduced too early to the very hard particles floating around in "room air."

It's human nature to save a dying thing. A veterinarian is called in for a pig or a cow, unintentionally wounded, even if the cow or pig is destined for slaughter. A little girl picks up worms that have been washed by the rain onto concrete and lay dying in the sun. She takes what half-moving parts she can and returns them to dirt. A woman swerves to avoid a chicken in the road. A man leaves dog food out for the elk after a hard winter.

A fetus born at twenty-three weeks sends into overdrive a human's usual intent to keep humans alive. As of right now, although advances continue to improve the health of prematurely born babies, very few babies survive being born before twenty-two weeks gestation. Many doctors don't think fetuses will ever survive born earlier than twenty-two weeks. Some don't think they should. But the scientists don't test these boundaries just as an experiment. They make it because breath compels them. About ten years ago, Dr. Gary Chan, a neonatologist at the University of Utah's Division of Pediatric Neonatology, was called to a delivery of a twenty-four-week gestation infant who was estimated to weigh less than two pounds. At that time, such a small, immature infant had a very small chance of survival. The infant was too small for their equipment. "We discussed this issue with the parents. When she was born, she required no assistance . . . she breathed normally! She weighed only 390 grams, one of our smallest infants who survived in Utah. She is doing well in Logan, Utah, and needs only glasses."

Here, the one good instance—the miracle—became an exemplar for the rest. If one kid could survive on her own, then with enough doctors, enough nurses, enough researchers, enough money, enough patience, and enough time, maybe all micropreemies can survive. And few parents, especially if they know it's possible for a twenty-two-and-a-half-weeker to survive, ever wonder if enough is too much. The individual hope combats the heavy statistics of despair.

To stop the contractions you have to stop everything. To stop time, you have to stop motion. You do not want this delivery to progress, so you suspend your disbelief that time-stopping is possible. The "you" here are the doctors. The "you" here is also the patient, and for now you have identical desires. If those desires diverge, you, the singular, will want to get up to pee. You the singular will want to unhook yourself from the IV, since the IV is delivering the magnesium sulfate. The main thing magnesium sulfate does besides try to stop contractions is to make your skin feel like it's covered with biting ants, which makes you want to leave the hospital, leave your bed, leave your skin, but you (the doctors and you) know you can't go anywhere. You the plural know it's best to lie down and take it. You the plural know not to complain, although the words going on in your head include motherfucker and who-did-this-to-me-in-the-first-place baby-blame, husband-blame, doctor-blame. What sadist even invented magnesium sulfate? But you stop. Stop yourself. You know it's good; it's for the best.

It's the hooking up that ties you down. Once they have an IV in you, you may as well lie back and enjoy the view. Usually, the view is of a corner television, hanging just high enough and far enough away that you have to twist your neck to see it. The remote for the TV is the same remote you use to move the bed up and down, and sometimes you manage to change the channel to the most-basic-of-cable-network options, and sometimes you accidentally move your bed so far forward that you're touching that stomach of yours, which you wish were higher or bigger, so that maybe they could give you a different drug that would get that baby out of there—thereby getting you out of there—but instead you let better judgment reign, knowing that you should appreciate modern technology and try not to complain out loud.

You were just on the verge of getting a handle on the fish, and then they bring in the pig. The magnesium sulfate isn't working. The contractions are increasing. You are barely six months into this pregnancy and had, on Wednesday, finally bought the first maternity clothes you might need since your sister had given you some stretchy pants, which is all you'd really needed until then, and, it turns out, all you really need at all. No *Motherhood Maternity* shopping for you. Now they're coming in with something called surfactant. Surfactant is made from calf lung or pig lung, beneficial for infants born at thirty weeks of gestation or less. The surfactant controls surface tension in the lungs, meaning that water that might stick won't. The air sacs, underdeveloped and stuck to each other, aren't supposed to inflate until forty weeks of gestation. They're busy doing their fish-like conversion of oxygen to red-blood cells. But surfactant spurs the air sacs on, lets them open. They shake off their watery existence and exchange it for a non-watery one. Less surface tension. That sounds like a good thing, and yet you are nothing but tension. They regale you with a list of consequences if this baby is born now—respiratory distress syndrome, which the surfactant will help; a chance of cerebral palsy, which the surfactant will not; an aorta that won't close; brain hemorrhages; sepsis. You don't want to hear any more. You want to go home to your stretchy pants. You want to go back to being the protector and the nurturer. You want to make the lungs have less surface tension. You want to prohibit, with your folic acid taking, any brain problems, including bleeding ones. You want not to know what cerebral palsy even is.

If there's one thing pregnancy will teach you it's that time does not go backward any more than gravity stops pulling, any more than knowledge unknows itself. Right now, gravity is pulling your baby down. You can feel your cervix. Unlike when giving birth at full gestation, you have the benefit of surprise to numb you. Your whole bottom half is lowering itself toward the ground without the help of a Craftmatic bed or buckling knees. Your body—and your baby—is on its own. You tilt the foot of the bed upward toward the TV, but not even that technology can save you.

In the United States, it's almost always a bad time to be a pig. In 1989, it was a particularly bad time to be a pig in the world of neonatology. This pig did some charitable work. Eighty percent of the decline in the infant mortality rate in the United States between 1989 and 1990, can be attributed to surfactant therapy, states an article in *Science Daily,* the year in which surfactant therapy was introduced.

Who would think to look at the surface tension levels in the lungs? Only those researchers focused on helping premature infants survive. But the helpfulness of the strategy didn't end there. A study involving nine infants with meconium aspiration syndrome, five adults with congenital pneumonia and one adult with respiratory distress syndrome, showed that surfactant improved oxygenation in twelve members of the study. Like the study on the relationship between placenta communication and autism, the surfactant-slurping babies aren't using all this research for themselves.

You, on the examination table, would thank the pig for its sacrifice if you knew about it, but you aren't too interested in the problems of lung surface tension at the moment. At the moment, you're just wondering who you can find to take you to the bathroom. You're afraid to go alone. You're afraid if you bend your knees to squat, you'll give birth right into the toilet. The baby will slide out, too small for you to even notice. You don't want to think that you've had periods worse than this.

Instead of taking you to the bathroom, the nurse brings you a bedpan. If a baby slides out, they'll be able to catch it before it gets swept away into the drain like any tiny goldfish.

You wish you didn't think so nimbly, so numbly, about such tiny things. There's a problem. In the hospital, you can't think anything except morbid thoughts. You think you'd be safe with all the protective coating around: white gowns dotted with tiny blue stars, plastic chairs, plastic tubes connected to plastic grommets connected to white hygienic-looking metal. And yet red thoughts creep in. You're lying down but you can't even pretend to sleep. An alarm down the hallway. Someone's dying. Code blue, code blue. Everyone is turning blue.

You could also speculate. You can play word-association games—speculate, speculum— and wonder why the doctor won't use a speculum to check to see if you're dilated. When you ask, the nurse tells you about a study that shows that metal speculae infect birthing patients more readily than nooked and crannied, wrinkled and scabbed, butt-wiping and eye-itching fingers. Speculate, suspicious. How could metal host more microorganisms than a finger? They can sanitize metal.

Bodies are best for other bodies, you used to think. Your uterus is where the baby is supposed to live. It's the best place for it. All the food and water the baby needs are pumped to the baby. The membranes between the outside world and the fetus are thick for a reason. They keep the bacteria and viruses out until the baby can build an immune system—until your body knows how to let the good ones grow on her eyelids, to keep them clean, and in her stomach, to digest food, and how to keep the bad ones out. Things will never be as ideal for her as in the womb, even if she is born on time. But she will not be born on time. She will be born today, just like you feared. She will be born at a time that was judged a miscarriage just a few years ago. Now, she'll be called a micropreemie, and you'll blame yourself, even if there's nothing you could have done. She will be thrust into an environment that was not at all meant for her—bright lights, cold metal, thick plastic, dry air.

You have been trying to think about fish. Or, rather, you've been trying to think about fishy frogs—the way they begin as fish and turn to fully animated frog lungs. Perhaps with enough of the pig fat, your baby could pump those fetal-lungs into the ballooning air sacs they are supposed to be. But when the contraction monitor starts blinking, all bets on positive visualization are off. If you were a landmass, and the belt around your waist was measuring seismic disturbances, the scale would be showing sharp peaks, close together. If you could equate contraction to earthquake strength, the fetal monitor would be showing an 8.8. When you later read about the Chilean earthquake that devastated the Maule Region of Chile, you will be reminded of the fetal monitor: 8.8 seems about right.

And so the scientists do what they always do when calculations top the charts—they intervene. "Natural childbirth" at twenty-four weeks is never natural. What set off this string of events is hard to say. Perhaps it was due to an amniotic-fluid infection. Perhaps it was due to congenital defects. Perhaps it was the fact that you tried so hard for two years to get pregnant, and whenever you try hard for something, even if you finally get it, it never stops being hard. You will always wonder what you did to make this happen. Perhaps future doctors will know why the mother's perfect environment stops being a perfect environment, why your body would thrust your baby into the imperfect world. Whatever the reason, the doctors found that the baby was coming, and there's no way to stop it now.

It was more of a slip of a fish than the push of a bowling ball.

Your baby is born at twenty-four weeks, three days gestation.

She weighs one pound, three ounces.

She looks like a baby in that she has two arms, two legs, a torso, a head. Ten fingers. Ten toes. But her skin looks alien—purple and covered with fine blond fur. If you lift her arm and peer at the hang of her armpit, the purple turns translucent. There should be more thickness between inside and out. The umbilical cord that had strung together a symbiotic relationship between mother and baby has been cut. Now the baby floats in the atmosphere without harness or host. Her skin, usually a first line of defense in full-term babies, is barely a membrane. Her lungs are closed rubber, tight as cord, thin as silk. Blow a spider's wink of air and the sacs collapse like webs.

Part of you, the part that is curious more than the part that falls in love, looks at the baby, almost as red and worn and angry-skinned as are your hands from washing again and again just so you can see your baby and part of you wants to run away. But you stay and wash against the germs with the same commitment with which you ate the crackers you hated in order to fight nausea and keep that fetus fed. You now know that these little gestures do add up. This baby would have no brain if it hadn't been for the hydrogenated fat in every Ritz cracker you ate.

She is specimen and fish and alien from beyond, but she adapts to this environment. The air sacs in her lungs, thanks to the surfactant, inflate like tiny balloons, puff up thanks to a continuous positive airway pressure (CPAP) machine that presses that wink of air in just the right amount of pounds per square inch (measuring more milligram than pound, more micrometer than inch). Her body responds to the heater, which keeps her a comfortable ninety-nine degrees when her internal thermostat cannot. A hundred different kinds of medical treatments have been invented for her. Drugs and surgeries to close her patent ductus arteriosus (PDA), a vascular connection between the heart and the lungs that naturally closes in full-term infants but sometimes fails to close in preterm infants. Ventilator tubes designed for very small esophagi are fed down her throat. IV lines with very small needles have been inserted into her veins, and very small feeding tubes have been laced through her nostrils, fed down the other pipe, into her very small stomach. She will be monitored for retinopathy, sepsis, bleeding on the brain, and necrotizing enterocolitis, where parts of the small intestine swell and die because immature intestines are more prone to infection.

Your baby was the perfect environment for the bacteria called *Enterobacter cloacae. Enterobacter cloacae,* in some environments, has the capacity to do a lot of good. It has been used in a bioreactor-based method for the biodegradation of explosives and in the biological control of plant diseases. Without oxygen, the microorganism can reduce selenite to selenium. Water becomes contaminated with selenite discharges from industrial practices such as fossil-fuel combustion, petroleum refining, and mining. Selenite is soluble, toxic, and can bioaccumulate in the food chain, but, as noted by the MicrobeWiki at Kenyon College, *Enterobacter cloacae* reduces it to elemental selenium, which is nontoxic and insoluble. High levels of SeO_2 in water have been identified as the cause of both embryonic deformities and the death of aquatic birds.

In premature babies, neonatal infection with *Enterobacter cloacae* can be fatal. In the NICU, two cribs down—isolated, thank god, by Isolette, trademarked name for incubator, a premature infant was diagnosed at day twenty-one with *Enterobacter cloacae*. Five cerebral abscesses were discovered six days ago. They treated the baby boy with the antibiotics cefotaxime and amikacin. The nurses will switch to axepim and ciprofloxacin during the next four weeks, if he makes it that long (fingers crossed), until cerebral abscesses regress.

You do not want a baby with abscesses. When other parents walk by your baby's Isolette in the nursery, you want to flap at them. Stay back, germ-carrier. You barely trust the nurses who are gowned and washed. Their hands are ravaged by the harsh soap and constant washing. Your own hands are starting to look like theirs. Road rash. As if you've been anywhere near a road since you checked in.

The doctors are concerned about your baby's hydrocephalus. They tell you they might have to perform surgery to install a drain to pull the water from the inside of her head. You look at your baby. At the baby. Is this your baby? Is this head so large because water plumps it large or is it large because your head is also large? She almost looks normal. Her face had looked almost as road-rashed as your hands. Now, days after her birth, it has turned as white as your niece's had been the day after she'd been born at full-term. Big, water-headed baby. Here in the NICU, it's always water. Washing your hands, fluids dripping through tubes, nurses and their big fat water bottles, sipping away from the babies, making you thirsty, you who forgot your cup. Too much water. No wonder you're always thinking about fish. This whole state is too full of water. Maybe if you'd had the baby in Arizona instead of watery Michigan, this big water-headed problem wouldn't be happening.

When you see a baby born at twenty-four weeks survive, and then you see, ten years later, another twenty-four-weeks gestation baby who needs some breathing help, who needs some surfactant, who needs PDA surgery and feeding tubes, how can you not give her everything medicine has? After seeing that girl survive with nothing, how can you not give more to this one?

Dr. Christian Yost tells the story of a twenty-five-weeker who adapted on her own. This baby girl was born right at twenty-five weeks, which just a few years ago was considered at the very limits of viability. After careful consideration and with tearful resolve, her single mother chose to hold her immediately following delivery rather than subject her to the painful and invasive process of life support offered by the newborn intensive care unit. Her mother received counsel suggesting that even with full resuscitation the odds of survival without death or severe disability were close to zero. So this mother chose to allow her daughter to pass away in her arms.

The baby girl, however, had other ideas. After eight hours, and although her core body temperature was low, she was still vigorous, breathing on her own, and making sucking motions on a pacifier. At that time the care plan changed, and she was given the benefit of all necessary therapies and treatments to support her growth and development. Her NICU course was long, probably painful, and definitely invasive, but very successful. She has thrived under the care of her mother since then. On the day that she visited our unit as a teenager, she reported that school was going well and how excited she was to have just received her driver's license.

You used to spend a lot of time at the lake. In Michigan, you can't not spend time at the lake. When you were seven, you walked too far into the reeds. Your feet got soaked. You cut yourself on a reed. You could hear your mother's voice calling you to come back, but you couldn't feel wet or pain or even see your mother. Under your right foot, before you put weight on it, you felt something less than rock, more than plant. You lifted your foot. Underneath was the speckled round shell of an egg. You didn't know what kind it was. You bent over to look more closely at it. You wanted it. You knew you shouldn't pick it up, but if you had been wet and cold and alone, you would have wanted to be picked up. So you put it in your hand. And there, you saw the hairline crack. What do you do with a cracked egg? You think of teacups you've broken and arms of dolls that have fallen off. You dream of Super Glue. You wanted the mother bird to flap its wings at you, to fight you off, to send you away. But there was no bird around.

You wonder if your baby is going to survive. If she does survive, will she be able to see? To hear? Will the water on her brain retard her? Will she be able to walk? These doctors opened the egg-shell and puffed air into this little bird's lungs, but god, will she fly? You wish she would have stayed a fish just a little bit longer.

An easy argument against saving these babies: all this money for so few individuals, is it worth it? The amount of money spent per year in the United States alone on premature birth is almost six billion dollars. Let's put it in perspective: three billion dollars have been spent on a recent attempt by the World Health Organization to vaccinate 575 million children. Another three billion dollars might eradicate polio entirely, even in Northern India where seventy-five percent of children remain unvaccinated. Those images of grown men rolling around on skateboards or carts because their legs have withered may disappear from our television screens entirely.

Six billion dollars could begin to dig into the Nigerian aquifer, one of the largest in the world, to bring water to people in a region where people die daily from lack of access to clean water. If you want to think locally instead of globally, six billion dollars could go toward curing breast cancer, one of the leading causes of death for women in the United States. Or think even more locally, and consider how six billion dollars could send every eighteen-year-old kid in Michigan to college for four years or buy 86,189 homeless people in Michigan a house (in Michigan). Six billion dollars toward premature babies adds up in the details. The book *Preterm Birth: Its Causes, Consequences, and Prevention* estimates the average cost of each preterm infant delivery and immediate medical costs in the United States is $51,600. But many births can end up costing millions over a lifetime. The direct cost for mental retardation can be $19,133. Physician visits; $3,513. Prescription medication; $30,151. Inpatient stays; $3,078 Assistive devices; $13,181. Therapy and rehabilitation; $54,185. Cerebral palsy, $83,169. Hearing loss, $23,209. Vision impairment, $32,058 over the duration of childhood. Expenses incurred when the preemie becomes an adult aren't calculated in this study.

Costs were highest for extremely preterm infants, averaging $65,600, and for specific respiratory-related complications. However, two-thirds of total hospitalization costs for preterm birth/low birth weight were incurred for the substantial number of infants who were not extremely preterm. Of all preterm low-birth-weight infant stays, fifty percent identified private/commercial insurance as the expected payer and forty-two percent designated Medicaid.

There are indirect costs, too, such as early intervention, special education, and caregiver costs, as well as lost productivity and labor in adults born prematurely who continue to suffer adverse effects. *Preterm Birth: Its Causes, Consequences, and Prevention* compiles these numbers to argue for more early intervention and education. The book argues more studies and more public outreach can help reduce these costs, but one can add up the costs. A twenty-three-weeker who is blind, has cerebral palsy, who has brain damage . . . well, the problem is, you won't know how it will turn out until you go ahead and save the twenty-three-weeker.

But if you want to think very locally, you can think about a tiny baby. If that baby is born, gasping for breath, no matter whose fault it is, you should intubate. Not necessarily because the outcomes will be good, but because who knows how this one baby will respond? If you can do it, the logic goes, you probably should. If you've seen one baby breathe one time, how can you not give another one a shot? At Children's Hospital Los Angeles, the nurses hung a photograph on the wall of a baby named Luke who had been born at twenty-three weeks. Because he was the earliest baby born at CHLA, they had marked his growth by inking and papering his foot every week. At twenty-three weeks, his traced foot was the size of a bee. At twenty-eight weeks, the size of a quarter. At thirty-two weeks, it had grown as long as a double-A battery. They did this until he was a year old, when his foot had reached the size of a regular baby's—about that of a mouse.

Although money is a common American gauge, it isn't the only one. Dr. Susan Weidermeier, another neonatologist working at the University of Utah, notes that although babies survive, they live whole lives with debilitating effects. "I am not certain that they ever really 'recover' their full potential. We are only beginning to understand the consequences of the epigenetic alterations induced by development in the NICU environment. The 'survival'-induced alterations of the human, preterm infant or other, do not come without a price."

One mom I spoke with said that she felt there was always something wrong with her daughter, who was born at twenty-five weeks. "She just isn't a normal kid. She doesn't exactly fit in the autism spectrum, but when she's in a crowded room, she just goes bonkers, bouncing off the wall." I wonder about the placental communication. If there's something the placenta plants inside a kid's brain that says, Hey kid, stop being so loud that preemie babies miss, having been separated from their placenta at such an early date.

The question of how much to devote to one individual intersects with how artificial and abnormal humans have made our environment—

the NICU is an extreme version of how we adapt our environment to suit our individual needs. The question Dr. Weidermeier asks—what is the price of what we've created?—is a large one. When does the saving, at any cost, of the individual life—thanks to our amazing ability to replicate (but never quite be) the human uterus—stop trumping other concerns, like quality of life, direct and indirect costs, global inequities, and social welfare systems?

As Dr. Yost argues that we have reached a plateau for the limits of viability. He's treated pre-term babies born before twenty-three weeks gestation. Each of them died. He believes that "until the next paradigm-shifting, technological adaptation, the current limit of viability should be respected."

The earlier example he provided of the girl who succeeded miraculously suggests that if one twenty-five-week gestation baby can survive on its own without extreme intervention, then intervention on behalf of other (now twenty-three week) babies is a worthy endeavor. The limits are defined by those surprising babies. His philosophical questioning of how much humans should press those limits also makes sense. Humans can make things adapt to suit them, but it's not always in their best interest. There are limits to adaptability. The baby's lungs can learn to breathe with surfactant. Her body can warm in an Isolette. The hole in her heart can be repaired with microsurgery. With extreme intervention, survival is possible, but perhaps a kind of survival that is sustainable. At some point "extreme" means everything. The nurses, doctors, and NICU are breathing for the baby, feeding the baby, warming the baby, cooling the baby, pressurizing the baby's blood vessels, pumping the blood, keeping the eyes wet, keeping the skin dry. Everything is adapted for the baby. The baby adapts by surviving.

Can doctors keep every outcome in mind simultaneously? It's not an entirely impossible request. Doctors remember many things at once—why not everything? Can a doctor imagine every tiny environmental shift that could be tried to increase the success rate of the preemie? Think of how we alter our environments ever so slightly, all the time. Your foot falls asleep. You stand up. You're hungry. You go to the kitchen for a banana. The question for the individual eventually becomes the question for the many. In different environments, you do better. Sometimes you need to move from one place to another—on to the porch, back to the couch, to the car, to Phoenix, to Detroit, to Los Angeles—to do well. Sometimes you have to put on your glasses and see the dirt on the windows. Sometimes you have to take them off to see how clean things are. Sometimes you have to make adjustments to where you are. If you're hot, turn the fan on. It ventilates.

Caring for preterm babies increases our understanding of the body's ability to adapt in general as well as in the tiny specific. As the study noted, the health care costs increase every week earlier a baby is born—meaning if doctors can keep the baby in utero one more week, costs can be reduced substantially. This is a good reason to continue to study micropreemies and a good reason to study prenatal health. But the repercussions don't end with the individual baby. Some of the research that has been devoted to decreasing preterm infant mortality and increasing efforts to keep the baby in utero has led to other advances that contribute to the broader population. These aren't even necessarily medical advances, but issues that run the gamut, from privatizing hospital rooms to complicating the abortion debate; from clustering care to mainstreaming special-needs kids; from women's health issues being brought to the forefront to calling attention to the fact that more African American women than White women give birth prematurely, as do women in poverty as do women who live in air pollution or in countries without neonatal intensive care units. The intense focus on these micropreemies has led to larger understanding of both our own individual bodies and our collective national health body. Collectively, the country fell into a depression when John and Jackie Kennedy lost their 34-week baby. Conversely, we read with exhilaration about the successful vascular surgery on a heart the size of a cashew. The preterm infant is a phenomenon. An expensive, groundbreaking, heartbreaking phenomenon.

You look down at your baby. It takes a while to love any baby in the same way it takes a while to love any alien. It takes a while to love an alien who has had heart surgery, eye surgery, who was on a jet ventilator, who had so much plastic contraption between you and it that calling it *it* didn't seem as cruel as it did accurate. But even twenty-four-weekers have hands. She reaches out to you. She curls her hand around your over-scrubbed finger, just like a regular, non-broken baby would.

The way the baby rubbed her tiny thumb against your index finger. The way she balled up her tiny fists, mad, even though she couldn't make any noise on the vent. The way she looked up into the light and blinked at it—suggesting that maybe she, too, could see. The way she stroked the arm tied down to tubes with her other free arm. The way her ears curled like a snail's. The way her belly pressed round as an otter. Her fingernails as sharp as any nails. She is fierce and lo, though she may have cerebral palsy, chronic lung disease, blindness, deafness, or, later down the road, a propensity toward adult onset hypertension, coronary artery disease, high blood pressure, her own struggles with infertility and premature birth—the amount of care that went into making that child live, the ways the fetus could adapt to living in such a plastic world, the kinds of adjustments and modulations, the sheer number of bodily processes that were done for her that she then learned how to do—she will be made out of these adjustments. She's the sign of the everything you have ever had to think about at once happening simultaneously.

She'll adapt, with a little help, thanks to a science that tries to understand what the womb is like in there and can make a virtual womb happen out here. And what you will be able to say about her is that she met the future head on, with a little help from the world coming out to meet her. In fact, she might even help all of us to understand what it takes to survive when thrust into environments we're neither physically nor temporally prepared for. She embodies a microclimate; she's lived in the most microclimatic environment of all. She's staved off microorganisms and learned to grow good ones in her gut. She's not so much a metaphor as an anecdote. An anecdote and a sign that signals the way minutiae matter.

◎

Microbortions

<Microbortion 1>

People always bring up math. A million fish in the sea. One million sperm, flushed. One million people starving somewhere near my backyard but not in it. One in a million possibilities—a green bird with a yellow beak. Call it pumpkin. Call it a nascent jack-o'-lantern with already a face. A girl playing basketball as the sun splashes into the sea. And then they take it down a notch. One in a 1,000. One in a 100. One in ten chances and nobody will cover the odds. At twenty weeks they saw something. At twenty weeks the bend in the spine, the crook of the neck, the shape of the nose, too many signs to add up to human. This imprint of a child who had not yet twisted her head toward breast, who knew only the stuff of fish—water, bob, gases, flip—came pre-broken. The world wouldn't have its chance to do its best to her. The only thing now was to wait—wait for the twenty more weeks, wait for the gasp or air, wait for the ventilator, wait for the mask, wait for the paralytics that kept her fins from flapping against herself, bruising her forehead, bluing her cheeks. The mother had always loved fish. She would spend her life regretting the ocean.

<Microbortion 2>

It attached to her uterus like a wad of gum under a table. It ballooned inside of her until her insides were more peppermint than blood. When she finally made it to the doctor, it was too late to remove the growth. Twenty weeks was the limit and even God could see she was pregnant now. At week forty, she tried to dislodge that wad with the force of a chisel. As the doctors tugged on the head, they pulled the woman inside out. Now, at the playground, she's stuck to the bench, stuck on her ass, stuck drinking Tab, smacking gum against gum against gum.

<Microbortion 3>

She loved the baby already just like she loved otters. She loved the baby already just like she loved the swell of her breasts, the frog of her belly, the clanking of her widening hips. But this baby couldn't be hers. Twelve-years-old. She loved otters. That's why she let them swim in the sea.

<Microbortion 4 >

She would pay for it. That's what they always told her. She would pay. And, since he wouldn't pay, she did pay, or tried to. She worked for tips. She sold her books. She gave someone a blow job for twenty-five dollars. She'd given them for more, for less, in the past. She added up the cash. She took it to the clinic. The clinic told her to keep her money. She'd need it for diapers. She took the money. She handed it to the he. Then, she reached up inside her vagina and gave the he the uterus, the fallopian tubes, the amniotic sac. She'd given more for less, before. As she lay on the floor, her sweater absorbing the blood, she remembered one good thing. But then it slipped away before she could grab hold of it. It didn't matter, anymore, anyway. Not like the handful of blood. That meant something. It meant all the world to the he as he held the throbbing it in his inexpensive hands.

<Microbortion 5>

Enough should be enough. The children were like barnacles. Multiplying. Sticky. She got pregnant every time she sneezed. As if she was in charge of dust in her nose. As if she were in charge of the sun in her eyes. As if she was in charge of the putting it in. No. She was just in charge of the taking it out. So she took them out. Sometimes full term. Sometimes preterm. But the boat. It was getting heavy. It was starting to sink. The men saw her. Instead of sticking their hands out to help her up, they stuck their dicks in her. They sat on her. They pushed her down, holding onto her shoulders. And then she went under. As the last air from her lungs (no one else's) pushed bubbles into their world, she wished she'd been fitted with a man guard, a chastity belt, a vagina that was part piranha. But instead, she'd been fitted with a working uterus, luscious lips, and a bad habit of forgetting to vote.

◎

Microkeratome

It was only when I turned thirty-three that I saw the bad dictators had finally started dying. It was only when I turned thirty-seven that I saw that all the bad dictators had been replaced by new bad dictators and things were as much on the verge of apocalypse as ever. When Kim Jong II died, North Korea launched a missile to remind the rest of the world that even the starving cry when the only salvation they believed in turned out to be a regular man who smoked cigars and drank cognac and ate foie gras with a reduction of blackberry demi-glace.

What do you do, besides make lame jokes, to get your mind off North Korea? In the winter, the flags of *Bouteloua curtipendula* bend forward in the wind. The grass is drought-tolerant, with good erosion control. It is a threatened species in Michigan. It is your job not to make a metaphor of this but you can't help it. What you see is this: the seedpods look like steps on a ladder. They rise up toward the wind. Better for catching wind than climbing. The grasses, blue flowers in spring, have devised a way out of here. You step on the blades like they'll take you somewhere but you crush them with your heavy foot and your misplaced sense of order.

Still. The purple and blue flowers, if you focus on them, if you stare at them long enough, they turn to blur, and you can obliterate almost every other sense of meaning. There are so few blue foods. You don't even think about eating them.

◎

Microbladder

No one likes the movie *Waterworld*. My friends Ander and Megan bought me a copy of a board game based on *Waterworld* but no one will play it with me. The logic is too squirrely—why do the smokers have so much gasoline? Why so many cigarettes these many years later after the continents have all been swamped? In what natural selection game can you turn from man to fish in a few short generations? Kevin Costner's physiological needs include limes but he has already evolved gills? Darwin would not play *Waterworld* either.

~

My sister and I traveled to New York City together. Before he died, my dad liked to take us on vacations—airplane or rented RV or sometimes boat—but this was the first time my sister and I traveled alone together. People kept giving us free things—a hundred bucks off a three-hundred-dollar sushi dinner bill. We ate quivery urchin and fatty tuna back when tuna was fat, a bottle of wine as we exited the shared cab, and, finally, two free beers apiece in the afternoon before we our flight left for home.

On the way to the airport, as we drove through Queens, I lay down on the backseat of the town car. I squeezed my sister's hand. She was trying to defuse the pain. A bladder full of two Heineken. If we had been near home, I would have asked to stop, but nothing feels as foreign as laying in the backseat of a Lincoln on the expressway, car abutting car, heading toward JFK with a bladder full of beer.

~

Still, I like the movie—the way I cannot go *there*. I cannot travel to *Waterworld*. It doesn't exist. There is no travel opportunity missing. There is no thing I can own. Water, malleable, moving, Protean, resists possession.

~

I took yet another plane, not even bothering to offset my carbon output by buying carbon credits, to Hawaii. This time, it was all of us: My sister, her husband, her son, my mom, her boyfriend Tom, my husband, and his parents. Nine of my one family on one airplane. We each used 1.6 tons of carbon to get there. (We could have bought our consciences clean at air travel offset dot com for $208.03. We didn't). Perhaps we could have driven to California where they also have beaches.

But instead, we went to Kailua and watched the volcano pour enough lava onto hot ground to make us think the world had enough hot stuff to power itself.

Later, we realized we would need snorkeling gear and that snorkeling gear was cheaper to buy than rent. We drove both rental cars to Walmart. I refused to go in. I boycott Walmart for all the reasons there are to boycott Walmart. I waited in the car. At least until I had to pee. I didn't think peeing at Walmart would infringe on my no-Walmart policy. I tried to pee on the floor a little, to let Walmart know just what I thought about them. I didn't buy anything there. I wouldn't even look around, but it was thanks to Walmart gear, the snorkel mask in particular, imported from China, that I saw that giant sea turtle swimming away from me. Thank you, Walmart. Thank you, China.

~

I can though take comfort in the movie's metaphor that there is a destination like *Dryland*. *Dryland* is the thing opposite what you already have. It's the dream of finding abundance through scarcity. A lime tree in the middle of the ocean makes you love lime more than water. Dry land, just a block of it, if you could find it, would give you everything you need. It would deliver all the earth for your individual human needs. You could find an old car. Go driving around the top which must be, in some way, the top of Mt. Everest. You could take comfort in the fact that if you spit or piss or blow exhaust on it enough, it will remind you of home and that you can stay on this new land that looks a lot like old land for as long as the water stops rising.

◎

Microclimates Lower Sonoran

It's the little details that are vital.
Little things make big things happen.
—John Wooden

Walking on sand. What do you want to see here? You want to see a road runner. Javelina. A saguaro in bloom. Coyote. But the desert is full of rumors. Rumors and cartoons—neither of which is thirst-quenching. The reality is your feet ache. The sand presses too hard on the arch. It isn't just the heat or the dry air that want you out of here. Even the sand tries to convince you to go home. But you step on. It's morning. It should be cool but you can still feel the heat of yesterday still permeating from the ground. Looking down, you hope sand is at least interesting. Specks of blue and green and red. Once upon a time there was a mountain here that fell down under the hammer of the sun. Or, once upon a time there was an ocean here piling up crystal gifts, blue and green and red, then abandoned. The water ran off with the clouds and left nothing but the lonely sun which is already stitching up your back. You wonder if you put enough sunscreen on. You wonder if there is enough sunscreen in the world.

There are saguaros here. Chollas too. Foreign cactus. Prickly pear, which you are familiar with, thanks to T.S. Eliot, thanks to Southern Utah, thanks to regular cactus that are paddles and close to the ground and act like plants, not trees. Saguaros in cartoons always have hats on them. One of their arms is always waving. Saguaros should not read human. They should be their own thing. You try to approach one, to see its ownness. Seams underpin thorns. There could be a person in there, hiding out from the sun, waiting to pop out and harass the coyote or the road runner. They look meaty. An investment of water and time. Saguaros can live up to 150 years. It can take seventy-five years to grow a side arm. They are native nowhere except to Arizona and Sonora, Baja California and a tiny part of U.S. California. Other states that boast them are pretenders. Their saguaros as contrived as a blue bird that says beep-beep and a coyote that tumbles over canyon cliffs and lives to chase that blue bird one more time.

The road to the desert from Flagstaff is a steep one with changes in scenery as severe as the changes in temperature. I know that if I look to my right in a few more miles, on a little hill in the median between the lanes of I-17 going up and the ones going down, the first saguaro asserts itself. My husband Erik tells our daughter Zoe saguaros look like people, and want to disagree, but the saguaro does look like he's the ambassador of the Sonora. These taller-than-human cacti are alien. I could use an invitation to plunge further into the valley. My friend Samantha calls it the Valley of the Shadow of Death, except no one makes a shadow. There is no shade.

Past that first saguaro, what had been occasional outpostings of ranches or occasional groupings of houses that could be compounds—militant, polygamist, communes—places where no infrastructure invited them, where septic tanks and generators dominate, become instead finger-reaches of settlements, growing from the palm of Phoenix's hand. Exurbs that were on their way to becoming suburbs until the recession hit. Now, cul-de-sacs, complete with gutters and sidewalks, await developers to build houses there. Or worse, houses on cul-de-sacs, with roads and gutters and sidewalks awaiting people who are never coming to buy them. It's a ghost town with no ghosts because there were never any humans to haunt them.

And yet, in Phoenix's East Valley, on the other side from where I'm coming down, on the side that I'm hoping to get to without traffic jam or car accident on my way to visit the desert, they're still building. I'm coming to look for burrowing owls anyway.

"They used to be along every canal bank and vacant lot in Chandler, Gilbert, and Queen Creek," said Randy Babb, a biologist with the Arizona Game and Fish Department. "Of course, now you can't find a vacant lot or canal in those areas. All of those habitats are gone…I don't think we have the fear that they will disappear, but like other animals, they've suffered in the face of land abuse." Burrowing owls burrow here. Native to this part of the desert, they've survived drought and heat and dust storm. They're not surviving development. Even though there are empty subdivisions all over Phoenix, the hope is that this new construction, in this part of town, will lure the buyers over. If the owls love it there, won't the people? Although burrowing owls are protected by Federal law, they're haven't reached endangered status quite yet in Arizona. Developers say that they call in wildlife control to move them before they bulldoze, but they see so many of them—it must be hard to take their protected-status seriously. But of course they see so many of them. Where they're bulldozing is the last place they live.

Queen Creek spokesman Marnie Schubert said the town's street and public works crews have not had construction delays due to owl sightings.

"We have had staff run into them while doing general work on washes or roadways," Schubert said. "When that happens, we have some experts come out and remove them. There has been little impact." I don't think I can believe her. The impact statements always come from people who like to smooth things over. Where bumps in the roads and owls in the burrows can't be felt by steamrolling impact-statement machines.

I don't know what I'm looking for when I look for owls. In the forest, where I believe that the owls I would see live in trees, I know to look for owl pellets, the bones and hair of disgorged mice. But burrowing owls—do they keep their disgorgement in their burrows? Do they fly up, out of the ground?

I'm not even sure I believe in these owls, since they're said to live near "Queen Creek." The only streaming water I've seen in Phoenix is the water put on display, canaled and championed by the Army Corps of Engineers who are so proud of their ability to make a four-million-person city in the middle of the desert that they don't even bury their Colorado River and Salt River re-directions out of the way of the sun's evaporating rays.

But apparently the creek and owl both still exist. "[The owls] are amusing to watch, more than anything," Bob Fox, co-founder of Wild at Heart, a bird rescue, said. "We've heard stories of people walking their dog, the dog gets a little too close to the burrow, and the owl will fly down and smack it on the head."

These tiny owls, only ten inches tall, even though they live below ground, lord over the landscape. When they're not nesting underground, they perch on fence posts, eyeing the landscape with the same sense of ownership as a gigantic barn owl.

These owls are good for the desert. They eat prickly pear and cholla cactus fruit, a behavior unique to burrowing owls. They also control the population of geckos and field mice. The owls line their burrows with and make nests from mammal dung. According to *Arizona Highways* magazine writer Jodi Cisman, "Researchers believe the dung helps control the microclimate of the burrow and might even attract insects for the owls to feed on." Not even waste goes to waste in the owl world.

Burrowed in for the day, full on gecko and mice meat, thanks to mammal dung, the owl is cool even on this hundred-degree day. The Sonora suits her, or rather, she has become suited to the Sonora. She thanks the people for the cows they brought—that mammal dung is the best insulator.

But, she can't thank the people for everything.

Of course, to *not* bulldoze over their burrows, you have to see the owls first. Here's something even I know about owls. They're nocturnal. So, in the morning, when the coffee's mounted on the dash of your Caterpillar D-9 you can sit back in the fully thick-cushioned seat, look out through the wide panoramic window, crank the air-conditioning, tilt the blade forward and down into the reflection of the morning sun. Can you see any owls with that much sun in your eyes? The owls are asleep. Everything's electronic nowadays on the Cat D9 anyway, even the ripper control. The tractor practically drives itself. Your job? To not spill the coffee and to make sure the ground is smooth, devoid of ridges and lifts, burrows and sinkholes. If the burrows become tombs, how is the bulldozer operator to know? Even if owls made noise, how could he hear them what with the comfortable operation stylings that include a standard isolation-mounted cab that reduces noise and vibration. The cab is pre-wired for a 12-volt or 24-volt entertainment radio and is equipped with two speakers, an antenna, and a radio mount recessed in the headliner, which is also pre-wired for a 12-volt communications radio. Breaker. Breaker.

We humans don't live in the desert like the burrowing owl lives in the desert. We don't make our homes underground. Most of the time, the houses look a lot like houses in the suburbs of Michigan, Indiana, California, Colorado. Two-storied, many-windowed, carpeted houses built tall to reach the sun. Dark, asphalt shingles, bent and layered, praying to the sun to set.

There are some adobe houses in the desert. Houses built close to the ground, sand-colored and sun-resistant. But, for the most part, traditional ranch houses dominate the scene. Michiganders, coming from their cold and treed climate, need something to be familiar. We are used to stairways and gabled roofs. We are familiar with the thermostat. In Michigan, we turned it up to seventy on the minus-fourteen-degree-days in January. What is the difference in turning it down to seventy when it's 114 degrees in July?

In the Sonoran Desert, there are houses above ground with pipes running to them from wastewater treatment plants where the water from the Salt River and the Verde River and the Colorado River and the aquifer are pumped and diverted and aerated and made as clean (even cleaner) as the Michigan water the one-time Michiganders are used to.

But should that water stop running, and at this rate it will, perhaps we can take a lesson from the owl. Dig deep under the desert sand to avoid the desert sun. Make a pact with the cactus and the prickly pear and learn to learn how delicious they are. If they don't prick us, we promise to scatter their seed. Find a good recipe for gecko and mouse. And learn the insulating powers of cow dung. I saw a cow wandering through the empty neighborhoods one day, gnawing on dried stalks of landscaping. Even if the rivers stop running and the aquifer dries, the cows will still produce.

Cows are like humans—they create their own ecology. When it rains in the desert—which it does, sometimes more than you can imagine, monsoon, tropical-like rains that explain flowering cacti and buffalo grasses—cows still march up and down the sagebrush-covered hills, tucking their noses under plants, trying to extract some calorie from the stubs of the gray-green plant. Their hooves dig deep ruts into the once-sand-now-mud. An hour later, the clouds move on, the sun comes out to bake the hoof-prints into place. If it rains again, the cows return and drink rainwater out of their hoof-made cups etched in the once-mud-now-glazed-pottery.

I look at the ground instead of in the trees for owls. I see cow pies as far as the eye can reach. But from out of the hollow behind the cow pie, I see a flutter. Something unburrows. It is day time but whatever this fluttering creature is, its impact is as hard as ground.

◎

Micromeria

Micromeria just means mint. Not even tiny mint. Lots of mint. Lots of kinds of mint. Mint. If you plant it anywhere, it grows like bamboo. My old boyfriend's dad, right before he moved from one house in Tigard, Oregon to another house in Tigard, Oregon, planted bamboo along the fence. The instructions for planting bamboo read, line a deep hole with black plastic, otherwise, the bamboo will grow unbounded, taking out fences, roses, tulips, small fruit-bearing trees, and uprooting foundations. My old boyfriend's dad did not like his neighbor. The neighbor had built the high fence without asking Roger how it would be for him. The fence blocked not only the sun but the sunset. He planted the bamboo without a bit of plastic.

Three miles away, safely in his new yard, he planted lavender. He planted lemon verbena, forgetting it was a member of the ever-large mint family. Now the bees cover his yard, rolling in the flowers, getting their backs all sticky with syrup. The smell permeates the walls of the house, even the small room in the back of the house, where my old boyfriend's dad counts out old vinyl records, age staved off age by multiplication. The house murmurs with the number of bees.

◎

Microbursts

1.

The ravens fly low through the trees. I believe they want a little of my hair. Like X-wing fighters, they seem to be targeting my head. They must think that I am water or at least a source thereof, or perhaps I'm just in their way, drinking my mason jar full of ice. I leave the jar outside sometimes. Maybe they'll take the bait.

2.

I shouldn't yell I shouldn't yell I shouldn't yell but why in God's name can't you wear other shoes. No two-year-old should be so adamant about wearing flip-flops. I don't mean to lift you up hard and put you down in your crib soft, but I didn't even say no, I just suggested that possibly, you might want to wear other shoes to play soccer or baseball or run outside without getting sand and rocks stuck in your sandals. You sit down in the dirt, getting your pants as dirty as your soles and take off your flip-flops every sixteen seconds to wipe off the sand and the rocks and then you put the flip-flops back on and run and trip and cry and blame me for letting you wear those stupid shoes.

3.

I got caught out. My hair is stupid swiveled. My skirt, drenched. You think the clouds are just teasing you but they are as big of assholes as I am. They wander by, you beg them for rain, they blow out of town without even letting loose one drop. And then the next thing you know, you and your computer and your book are outside. It looks pretty clear, except for that one cloud. You type a sentence, copy a passage, drink from your Mason jar. And then out of nowhere, you are swimming in your own stew, a combination of misplaced trust and self-deprecation. You would run from this downpour but you've been asking for it, you know. Plus, you too, who were insistent on dumb shoes, cannot run away from this storm wearing flip-flops, taking cover under ravens.

◎

Micro Prairie Dogs &
Micro Turkey Vultures

Seventy days it hasn't rained. It's a record but when I turn on my tap, the water still runs. On the drive home from Kayenta, horses were licking the side of the road, hoping whatever had spilled from that Ford F-150 ahead spilled something lappable.

Nearer to my house, the prairie dogs run into the road. My daughter Zoe screams when she sees them on the yellow lines. They pile upon the stripes, for some reason. Perhaps they think, as I do, that massing together brings rain. Maybe they're trying to cover up the yellow that is obviously preventing the black monsoon clouds from letting go their water. Maybe they are trying to get to the other side, where the houses have hoses. The yellow lines bar them from access.

I should bring a bowl of water to them, although that may be somewhat like littering—big pink bowl in the middle of the prairie dog town. And I'm no scientist. I shouldn't interfere with their ecosystem. And yet, I already am sucking up all their water through my pipes. I water the daisies with them. Daisies from Mt. Shasta who somehow think this desert-living isn't so bad, as long as you have a Nicole to tend to you.

I still might take the water to the prairie dogs just like I still might take the chicken drumsticks that have gone bad in my refrigerator out into the woods. I worry that the vultures might get salmonella but I'm pretty sure they're stomachs are prepared for rotten chicken. I worry more that they may become reliant on my chicken delivery service and next week will start amassing on the fence. I'll try to go running through the gate with my dog and they, sensing no chicken, will find Nicole meat tasty enough. Or they'll at least look at me with their turkey necks. Chicken-loving cannibals. So instead I throw the chicken in the garbage. Five chickens died for those ten legs. And now the vultures are hungry and the prairie dogs are thirsty, so I have a glass of wine, turn away from the forest, turn away from the prairie dog town, look at the sunset, look out to sea, and save some water.

◎

Micro Snow Leopard

ounce[1]

<u>noun</u>

1. a unit of weight equal to 437.5 grains or 1/16 pound (28.35 grams) avoirdupois.
2. a unit of 480 grains, 1/12 pound (31.1 grams) troy or apothecaries' weight.
3. a fluid ounce.
4. a small quantity or portion

   Origin: 1350-1400; Middle English *unce* < Middle French < Latin *uncia* twelfth part, inch, ounce, derivative of *unus* one

ounce[2]

<u>noun</u>

1. snow leopard.

   Origin: 1300-50; Middle English: *unce* lynx < Anglo French; Old French *once*, variant of *lonce* (erroneously taken as *l'once* the ounce) < Vulgar Latin *luncea, derivative of Latin *lync-* (stem of *lynx*) lynx

I don't know how it happened. I was reading online about snow leopards and how they're losing habitat, and, now worse, the tree line, the actual place where trees can grow, is moving up, thanks to you-know-who (Voldemort, global warming). The snow leopard finds the heavy fact of trees non-negotiable. He prefers the liminal space of snow and sky. Snow leopards have been on the verge of extinction since Peter Matthiessen's great book where he tracks the snow leopard through the Himalayas where he meets many lamas, where he never sees a snow leopard. A whole book of never finding. A whole world of too much finding. While I'm reading about leopards, about lynxes, I'm also looking up micro words, as I do every day. I clicked twice. At dictionary.com I learn that another name for snow leopard is ounce. How we pronounce our deaths. No one can take it all at once. A draught of tar a day. An aspirin an hour. A sip of petrochlorate in the water. I am done. I am done, I say every day. I do not think I can do this any longer. This living slow. This slow dying. This world squeezes out snow or leopards ounce by ounce. The snow leopard, unfound by Peter Matthiessen, does not exist already. He is a figment, smaller than an ounce. He moves as tree lines move—through hair, and ounce, and lynx and shift. If no one bothered looking, he'd be safely splitting the difference between *ouns* and *unce*. He'd be throating the vowels. Coughing up the narrow split. He'd be middle English, middle passage, middle-aged. He'd be done, he'd say every day. Done lynx. Done ounce.

@

Microorganisms

January in Phoenix and, of course, it's not cold. It is sixty-five degrees outside. I'm wearing short sleeves. I'm also wearing a scarf to assimilate better with my interview subjects when they bundle up to go outside into what in Flagstaff we would call balmy but in Phoenix they call winter. Either way, it is just the right temperature for a scarf and a shirt and there is just the right amount of security for an expensive building housing Level-3 biohazards. This place is clean. Stainless steel and glass, concrete floors and metal handrails, not a single uninvited microorganism in the place. Lots of invited ones though: *Enterobacter cloacae*, salmonella, and anthrax to name a few. The CDC, were the Biodesign Institute to stop photoscanning security passes, would pull its funding and all the work on anthrax would come to a complete stop.

But I'm not here to hear about anthrax. I want to hear good news. Tired of reading about Gulf Coast oil spilling, natural gas fracking, water polluting, and globes warming, I'm looking to hear about repair. Bruce Rittmann, Director of the Center for Biotechnology came to collect me. I hope that Bruce might be able to offer me something—a catalyst, a rescue rope, a stimulus package—to stop the cascade of bad news, but I don't hold out a lot of hope. Still, Bruce promised to regale me with stories about wastewater treatment plants, and if that didn't sound like a story about saving the planet, I don't know what would.

I have a hard time believing in heroes. To me, they are as unlikely and non-extant as aliens, unicorns, and the promises of Oil of Olay. But non-existent and nearly-invisible are not the same things. Things are visibly wrong. The air is thick with smog. The water, even when it runs clear, is riddled with man-made chemicals. Bruce would introduce me to organisms that are mostly invisible. Maybe, to be a good hero, you had to be mostly invisible.

A fixer is a kind of hero and, although I might not believe in heroes, I do believe in rehabilitation. Here, at the Biodesign Institute, I'm going to try to understand how these tiny beings remedy that dirty air and that toxic water. Remedy is a human metaphor. The water and the air don't care what rides in their waves or on their winds. To them, they're not broken. It's from a user-based perspective that things have gone wrong. What Bruce shows me is that usefulness can be reoriented. To a microorganism, chemical-ridden water is as user-friendly as a vending machine.

The tiny lesson I will learn here: microorganisms can restore water to its original self, hero-like and non-metaphorically. The big, metaphorical lesson: perspective shift and adaptation can make almost anything user-friendly. If that vending machine neglects to unwind your Cheetos, you can finagle a tool to encourage the spindle, spend another four quarters, shake the machine, call the manufacturer. You can adapt to this bad situation. And like you, microorganisms adapt to their surroundings and use them to survive, even thrive.

Bruce will take care of me, but I have to wait for the fix. Instead of wrapping me in the comforting story about things getting better, I first have to hear about things getting worse. Bruce chaperones me upstairs and hands me over to Rolf Halden, professor at the School of Sustainable Engineering and the Built Environment. Rolf, in the middle of preparing a talk to present to Congress, has been focusing on Superfund sites and cross-referencing them with hospital visits. Rolf takes me back downstairs toward bad news and lunch.

Arizona State University Organic Café

"So what do you want to talk about?" Rolf is obviously German. His accent as much as his first name make it obvious. But it's his locution that I find particularly attractive. There's such formality and precision in his voice but he's smiling the whole time. He smiles even as he tells me that when he worked at Johns Hopkins he studied newborn babies, finding manmade chemicals already polluted their newborn bodies.

"One hundred chemicals found in the babies before they have even taken their first breath. One hundred man-made chemicals can be found in the breast milk of 99.9% of mothers."

I think of Max, my son, and the breast milk I just weaned him from. I thought I had been doing him a big favor, nursing for a whole year. I thought I'd been promoting his good health, developing a stronger immune system, preventing allergies—all the things breastfeeding for one year is supposed to do. Instead, apparently I'd been dumping chemicals into him like he was the Cuyahoga River.

There are old wives' tales about what not to eat while breastfeeding: onions, garlic, thyme, chocolate, tea, raspberries, and honey. And then there are the more American Medical Association-approved proscriptions against smoking and drinking. But no one had told me, because old wives never knew and doctors don't track environmental contaminants, that I shouldn't eat out of my non-stick pans, drink out of the carton, or smear organic butter because the chemicals that coat our pots, line our milk cartons, and cling to our vegetables don't degrade. Chemicals stick around, persisting in our produce, our water, and, particularly, in our breast milk. Lipids, or fats, are great carriers of chemicals. If it's in the water or in the butter then it's in your boobs. If it weren't so Frankensteinian sounding, it would be kind of cool to have breasts full of chemicals. Spider? Zap. Out shoots some DDT. Milk-and-insecticide-covered-dead spider. And yet, as far as I know, there are no cartoon superhero women who shoot venom out of their nipples, although perhaps I shouldn't count out the Japanese on this one. Perhaps in American graphic art, expulsion from the nipple upsets the image of the nurturing mother. But doesn't too the image of the nurturing, nursing mother pouring contaminated lipids into her baby's mouth?

"Rolf. I've been poisoning my baby."

"No, no. It's still the best thing you can do for your child. All that immunity. You're protecting him from the environment he'd be introduced to anyway. And it's not like the chemicals aren't found in formula or cow's milk. That's what I mean by pervasive." But pervasive isn't the only problem. Finding the right tool to combat the myriad of pervasive contaminants in the water and soil is a lesson in making tiny decisions all the time. Microbiologists are as picky as farmers. One of the microorganisms used to clean toxic selenate out of water, *Enterobacter cloacae,* is also a notorious contaminant in infants and can kill babies born prematurely. Sometimes one microbe is a fixer. Sometimes a microbe is a killer. It's entirely dependent on the application. Which is why, I guess, Rolf is picky about where we went for lunch.

Rolf wonders, as we walk, if we should try our luck at the Thai, Indian or American restaurants. He rolls his eyes at all three, saying, "They're not that good. Cheap. Meant for college students. "Let's see if the organic restaurant is open."

We're in luck. Even though the university is between semesters, the café is open.

"You like sushi?"

I nod. "Spicy tuna rolls."

70

Rolf orders the sushi, a sandwich for me and one for him, a big salad for us to share. This is how Rolf is picky: he chooses everything and then takes a bite out of it to decide if in this particular application this sushi is good, this sandwich, this salad.

The server says hello to Rolf and pats him on the back like Rolf is an old friend. I gather, from the way the server brings us lemon for our drink and extra napkins without asking, that they *are* old friends, or at least that Rolf visited his local-organic-restaurant often. His kind of place, he thrives here. You can tell Rolf is a clean-living kind of guy. He works out. He doesn't put toxic chemicals into his body, if he can help it. Which, according to him, no one can help. But he isn't supercilious or sanctimonious. Perhaps Rolf has to be gregarious and open-minded if he's going to immerse himself in the contaminants of the world and try to find the one right microbe to combat one of the contaminants. Rolf put himself out there, in the world, at Superfund sites, at the wastewater treatment plant, at the restaurant and opened his arms to say—come to me. And in so doing, he found the perfect microbe, a helpful server, and a delicious salad and sandwich, even if the sushi was only so-so.

Brandywine Creek, Delaware

All this eating. All this talking. As Rolf tells me about Teflon polluting in the water system, I think about the non-organic salad I ate yesterday. It pollutes: fifteen known contaminants in the lettuce, the carrots, the beets. Rolf makes me feel like one big sponge. The body becomes a microcosm for everything that happens in the water, the food, the world *out there*. Bodies are places. Inside them, chemistry happens, DNA replicates, toxins reside. When I was nine, I put together a model of the Invisible Woman. I loved the bones the most, but I also loved the way the veins splintered and gathered and returned to arteries looked like a map of the rivers. I loved the idea of the Continental Divide casting rivers toward the east and rivers toward the west like a good heart organizing its oxygenated emissaries further and further toward the left and right hands of the coasts. I liked, then, the idea of everything being connected. Rivers are to veins as hearts are to watersheds. But in this version of the world, all that interconnectedness isn't the relief, it's the tension.

People put substances into places. The idea of "putting" something somewhere seems so intentional. If someone were to go out of their way to take, say, Teflon into a syringe and shoot it into a baby they would be arrested. Maybe go to jail. And yet the way Teflon rides through our consumer ecology mirrors the way Teflon rides on the water systems. Someone made it (culprit), but someone else wanted it (culprit), and someone else bought it (culprit), and some FDA official approved its nontoxicity (culprit). It's easy to blame a man with his hand on the plunger of a syringe. It's hard to blame the woman who wants to flip an omelet with one hand because she's pregnant with one baby and holding another baby on her hip. Even the chemist, who seems easily cast as the villain, is hard to blame directly. The chemist finds Teflon accidentally and now the woman flips omelets in her kitchen. The chemist shakes his beakers in a lab. The graphic designer draws pictures of beakers and kitchens in Adobe Illustrator in his office, three floors down from the marketing manager who will make a PowerPoint presentation to illustrate the new, cool kind of Teflon that can even withstand the nick of a metal utensil. These people never meet but their needs eddy and swirl, contribute to the river that becomes something like a necessity. Have you ever tried to scrub stuck-on scrambled eggs off a non non-stick pan? You might as well throw the pan away and what good would that do already-overflowing landfills?

In 1961, Marion Trozzolo, a chemist who had been using the substance on scientific utensils, came up with the advertising campaign for the new line of cookware, "The Happy Pan." And if you think of the last nonstick pan you tried to scrub burnt eggs from, you too would call this the Happy Pan.

Of course, it is not all happy. When a substance leads to practical, making-life-easier products, it pervades the marketplace as surely as the residue from manufacture pervades the river system. Teflon flows from the confluence of the Christina River and Brandywine Creek in Wilmington, Delaware. The Teflon runs-off from the Dupont labs and follows the Christina River to the Delaware River into the Delaware Bay.

These are not hideous rivers turned sulfurous and soupy. The water looks clear. The rocks seem rocky, no noticeable damage pockmarking them, dissolving them, melting them. There are no rows of dead fish lining the banks. Like most water, it appears entirely clean. It's see-through. Trees hover over the Brandywine. The leaves turn red in autumn but not chemically redder than the maples turning in Vermont. The water meanders toward the Delaware like it has for hundreds of thousands of years. The rocks move by millimeters. Turtles dig mud holes. Tadpoles swirl in eddies. This is a regular river that has regular water, at least in the sense that regular water now has Teflon flowing alongside it. Slippery rocks.

Teflon, applied to different products, is packaged up and carried out, where its residue finds its way into the water not by manufacture but by utility. Teflon flows on the backs of trucks and in the boxcars of trains, like a well-integrated, multi-directional river, west toward Oregon and southeast to Texas and due south to Oak Ridge, Tennessee. The Teflon goes on and on, across the sea to China where they now make the pans and then ship them back to Delaware where Walmart sells the T-FAL Basic Nonstick Easy Care 10" Covered Fry Pan for $16.97. T-FAL stands for Teflon. Teflon stands for Perfluorooctanoic Acid, for short, PFOA.

Substances slipping past places like rivers, even if they don't stick there, do stick somewhere. Perhaps reside in is a better word choice. Reside means to make a home in. It suggests permanence. Coziness.

Safely ensconced in. A settlement. No one is relocating Teflon or PFOAs out of their newfound homes. PFOA settles in breast milk but it's just one of many manmade chemicals that reside in bodies. Titanium oxide, used in toothpaste, is found in frogs. Triclosan, one of Rolf's most current projects, persists in solid waste. Rolf tracks the PFOAs, the titanium oxide, the triclosan. Kris McNeill, a friend from college who is now a professor at the Swiss Federal Institute of Technology (ETH Zurich), published an article on how sunlight chemically converts Triclosan into dioxin in rivers. Ingesting dioxins is known to increase cancer risk. Warnings about eating fish from the dioxin-filled San Francisco Bay abound even though you love fish, especially when you're in San Francisco.

Rolf spends a lot of time collecting samples from sewer systems across the US. The problem is, the FDA is interested in the cleanliness of water but Triclosan persists only in solid waste. Solid waste the FDA considers inert. Because it can be moved away from the community of wastewater-users, the FDA designates it fully resolved. But those biosolids from waste treatment plants are trucked somewhere to dry. In the US, we imagine that "over there" is safely distant from "over here." But when the winds come, the chemicals from the solids are blown over crops or onto grazing land where cows nibble, digest, incorporate the Triclosan into their muscles. Their delicious muscles that humans go on to eat. The "over there" moves "over here" with the help of the planet's big circular systems—wind and water. There is no over there.

Triclosan is one of the anti-microbacterial agents found in anti-bacterial soap. You can also find it on sports equipment and in deodorant, in carpet, rulers, and pens. My pencil sharpener claims to be anti-microbial. All those kids from my daughter's school covered in germs. I can see the attraction.

"It seems like a good thing," Rolf said, "no bacteria. But we're beginning to suspect that it's one of the causes of food allergies. It harms microorganisms in the gut biome. We don't even know each of their names. But think, every time you wash your hands, you eventually put something that you touched into your mouth. The antibacterial soap reduces the microbacteria in your gut. Our immune systems. We're weakening them every day."

Our fear of the invisible, or the nearly invisible, coupled with our fear of contagion, and the heaped-on fear of anything that shows dirt, and you can see why the woman shopping for groceries has Pantene and Pinesol, Dial and Glad garbage bags, and a plastic cutting board in her cart. The germs are coming. She collects the arsenal that will protect her family.

I have my own germ phobias—when I'm not busy ignoring dog hair and piles of old laundry. I panicked fully during the swine flu epidemic. I vacillate between believing the studies that show the French are in better health because their immune systems are better balanced by the refusal to employ Lysol and my mother who says, even if her house is messy, that it's "clean." Clean meaning antiseptic. Clean meaning you can eat off the floor and not get sick, even if you don't have the immune system of the French. I am a spectacle of contradiction. I keep sponges for weeks rotting in the sink but I also rub the handle of the shopping cart off with the Clorox wipes Safeway offers at the door. I will use my daughter's toothbrush but if my toothbrush falls on the floor, I will dip it in Listerine before I brush. There is no restroom too gross for my wussy bladder but I squat to pee at bar bathrooms as well as in the forest.

But Rolf raises the question, what if the antibacterial soaps and antimicrobial pencil sharpeners do more harm than good? What if the arsenal the Lysol-loving mom sprays on every surface piles chemicals more dangerous than any well-lived-with germs? Hygiene is a good thing—running water and soap have transformed houses, restaurants and bathrooms from bastions of disease to bastions of sanitation. Perhaps the idea of "soap" has been taken too far. Celiac disease? Irritable Bowel Syndrome? Weakened immune system? Are these diseases that you might have avoided if you'd been a better host to those internal microorganisms? If you recognized that your body is a wastewater management system, then you would know that healthy systems are made with the help, not the obliteration, of microorganisms.

My Backyard

Rolf pointed to the dessert he bought—some sort of coffee ice cream frozen into a tiny creamer and some ginger-crusted profiterole. He motioned for me to take a bite. I felt secure there, surrounded by organic food, a sustainable building and Rolf's insistence that we can figure out how to make this work, like it wouldn't kill me to enjoy myself a little—stop thinking about polluted breast milk and eat a little dessert. I could tell Rolf had a sense of balance. He could bring the bad news but then still eat a smorgasbord. Maybe he was just trying to stimulate his gut biome.

"Do you have a degree in chemistry?"

"No, biology and engineering."

"And yet you spend so much time with chemicals."

"Well, that's why I'm trying to make them green. My biology and engineering degree conspire to make me make sure things turn out good."

The idea of Green Chemistry isn't new. Paul Anastas, a one-time employee of the EPA, and John Warner developed the principals of Green Chemistry—a chemist's version of the medical doctor's "First do no harm." The argument for green/sustainable chemistry is similar to the argument for all kinds of sustainability: Use as little energy as possible. Clean up after yourself. Make sure that you use all parts. Don't use corrosive agents. Use renewable feedstock. It's a lot like the model of whole animal eating: kill the pig quickly and cleanly and humanely. Eat the ears.

As Rolf tracks Triclosan and studies its effects and works with Congress, he goes forward with the mission to persuade drug companies to embrace Green Chemistry, by which he means follow your chemical to its end state, make sure that when it's done doing what it should do that it doesn't bind with other molecules and disguise itself as clean or eddy around in rivers or isn't stockpiled in biosludge where it's shipped off to the desert or the outlying agricultural lands where it becomes part of the soil and the soil becomes part of the plant and the plant becomes part of the cow and the cow becomes muscle we eat and the PFOAs and the Tricolsan and the hundreds of other chemicals become a part of us. Like wind and rivers, he argues chemists should make sure the circularity of chemical systems ends in equanimity.

Although Rolf doesn't study one place, he does think about the consequences of chemistry in terms of place. He thinks about the consequences of all "progress" in terms of place. "If we lived like humans once did, in small villages where everyone could see what everyone else was doing, there would be no Concentrated Animal Feed Operations, no nuclear power plants, no landfill, no sewage system. Our neighbors would not like those industries to be their neighbors. We could see what goes down, what effluent flows into the rivers. We could smell the landfill, the sewer, the CAFO." We'd also have very little beef in our diets, less electricity for our laptops and a lot fewer of the bad microbes living in our garbage and our sewage, because we could smell it before we could see it. NIMBYism is one of the most destructive human sentiments. Because we can ship our shit far beyond our backyards, we don't think about what is in the shit. If we had to live with our garbage, we'd make sure it didn't smell bad. The poet Diane Ackerman wrote, "Our cerebral hemispheres were originally buds from the olfactory stalks. We think because we smelled." Perhaps if we smelled more often, we'd think more often about what made that smell stink.

Change the sensory input from olfactory to visual: If you expand the lens and zoom out, the water that flows from the landfill is the same water you drink. The water that feeds the cows becomes embedded in whatever meat you eat. There is no new water. All the water is the same water that's been always here. It's getting older and heavier and more laden with toxins and it flows from east to west, rains from west to east, it cycles and spools like a gigantic wastewater treatment system.

Wind and water make everyone and everything, including your waste, your backyard.

But the problem with everything and everywhere—it becomes nothing in your mind. It's too big and too pervasive. It's like trying to talk about language without using words, just hand signals. That water is inside you as much as it "in nature." You can look outside on your human-planted trees and believe that this is nature. And it is natural. It was natural for you to want plants. It's natural for plants to grow, with enough imported water and nutrients, where you plant them. It's natural to look outside and sigh contentedly that you don't live next to a landfill, a coal plant, a silicon chip factory, a gypsum, gold, or copper mine, an oil refinery, a nuclear waste dump, a concentrated animal feeding operation or its attendant slaughterhouse.

The bad news is you do live next to all these toxin-emanating, resource-processing, industrialized plants. They're bringing their effluvia to a neighborhood near you.

When I was fourteen, sitting by the swing set at Sugar House Park, watching my boyfriend smoke, I pulled the grass up gently so I didn't break the root. Pulling each blade between my teeth, I drew a little milky cellulose like I was drinking from a straw. It felt industrious, getting something useful out of ornamental lawn. My mom, if she ever caught me, would have yelled at me not to do that. It was disgusting. Not just the goose poop but the pesticides. The park's pond sat at the bottom of Emigration Canyon, where the Mormons had first entered Salt Lake Valley, where now septic systems lined the banks, where silver ore had once been mined, where oil now seeps into the river, closing the canyon, forcing the city government to close Sugar House Park where the river flowed into man-made ponds.

Now, when I eat my Swiss chard, I think about the ground the chard was grown in or the reservoir that watered it. Sometimes, the Swiss chard tastes saltier than other times. Sometimes it even tastes metallic. Compared to the Swiss chard I eat from farms that grow their vegetables near Superfund Sites, the grass I ate at that park had been purer. I miss that milkiness now.

Your Stomach, USA

To understand microorganisms not generally but specifically is to understand how each one works and how each one works in unique environments.

This is why oil-eating microbes undid some of the damage done by the BP Gulf Oil Spill. This is why the same microorganism that creates a dangerous biofilm build-up on the interior of a pipe in a wastewater treatment plant might turn superhero when it reduces a particular astringent man-made chemical pooling up anew in the Cuyahoga River. Take an antibiotic, kill the microflora in your gut. It takes years to rebuild that microflora. In the meantime, you wonder why you're suffering from hemorrhoids, why you just can't eat spicy foods like you used to, why you get stomach cramps when running. There's even some evidence that an upset balance of microflora in your stomach can lead to colon, stomach, and prostate cancers.

After lunch, Rolf takes me to meet Rosy, officially, Dr. Rosa Krajmalnik-Brown. She and her graduate students are attempting to catalog the thousands of microorganisms that abound in your stomach. Dr. Rosy has found correlations between gut flora and autism. Rosy's team compared kids with autism to kids without and noticed that the gut flora of autistic kids was very different to the flora of normal kids. "We know there's a link between the GI and autistic behavior, and when the microbiology is handled a little bit, they are still autistic but their behavior improves significantly," she tells me.

Microbe maladjustment in the gut might not only be a contributing factor in the behavior of autistic kids but also in the cause of autism itself. Scientists link auto-immune disease, celiac disease, and rheumatoid arthritis to inflammation in the cell walls of pregnant mothers. This inflammation inhibits and interferes with the placenta's ability to communicate soothing hormones to a growing fetus. In an August 25, 2012 *New York Times* article that links inflammation, microbes, pregnancy, and autism, Moises Valaquez-Manoff writes, "And really, if you spend enough time wading through the science…an ecosystem restoration project [of the womb]…not only fails to seem outrageous, but also seems inevitable."

Dr. Rosy's team also looked at groups of obese patients, patients who had gone under gastric bypass surgery, and patients who had always been thin. "The bacteria that is present in obese patients, together with other microorganisms, form teams that are more efficient at getting all the energy out of the things that come into the intestine." The teams of microorganisms in the obese patients don't let any food go to waste—they store it as fat, whereas a thinner person's microorganisms let some of the calories from the food go—an argument against efficiency. The inefficient body lets more calories pass through the system unused—possibly because the microorganisms are in better balance with each other. Less stressed, they don't see every instance of food as a sign of future scarcity. "I'd better store up, just in case," says the stressed out, lonely microbe. The happy microbes are like, "Dude, there will be more where that came from. Let's hang out and dance around instead." These are very relaxed microbes.

My friend, Gabe Brandt, who works as a chemist and microbiologist at Johns Hopkins wrote me again to say, "There's an Armenian guy at Caltech who has some nice stuff on how the composition of bacteria in your gut correlate strongly with Crohn's disease— he makes some nice points about how there are ten times as many bacterial cells in your body than there are human cells. Also, the number of bacterial genes in your corpus relative to your own is like a thousand-fold higher. And there are numbers of species of bacteria whose sole habitat in the universe is inside the guts of mammals." We are more bacteria than our own genetic material. When Whitman claimed he contained multitudes, he understood the gut biome.

We don't tend to think about the stomach as a place. It doesn't seem that nice of a place to live. Microorganismsare much more flexible in their habitat. They enjoy the vicissitudes of the stomach. Their scenery changes every day. The canopy of broccoli florets, a sea of blueberries, geysers of Sprite, waves of wine, dune of pretzel, the lush partnership of yogurt. The gut flora make their home in a highly acidic, ever-shifting landscape. They have learned to adapt to you. You have adapted to them. In fact, you both grew and adapted together. A partnership of environments that lets you eat raw meat and somehow to continue to sit at the dinner table while the microorganisms do the hard work of calming e. coli, and making friends with salmonella. As you get up to stretch, your internal planet stretches with you. You respire and all the little beings are rewarded with new oxygen. They continue their good work.

The same microorganisms that rot meat are the same ones that age prime rib. Cheese, nicely sealed in its rind, relies on microorganisms to give it taste. Once that same cheese is exposed to air, it begins to turn to mold. Microorganisms in your soil can give you tetanus but other microorganisms in your soil allow the seed you planted to germinate.

I feel about microorganisms like I once did about maggots. I used to think that maggots were generally disgusting and worth exterminating until I saw them applied to a wound where they proceeded to eat all the necrotic flesh.

Gulf of Mexico, Louisiana

Biofilm is another word for slime. Microorganisms accumulate on the edges of wet lips—of pipes, faucets, bathroom corners, the creases behind stoves. Organisms pile up on these lips, living off the other slimy things that grow there like chemicals or other bacteria. This thin film of slime is slippery. It's the stuff of germs and sludge. It is the stuff you usually want to eradicate and eliminate. Do stuff to it with long "a" sounds. "Take." "Away." "Hate." You want to get rid of the slime. The gunk. Slime forces long "ew" sounds: Lubricant. Lewd. Drool. Rude. Stool. Pool. Booger. Accumulate.

Bruce, even though his name has the "ew" sound in it, isn't himself slimy. But he does attend *to* slime. Bruce is balding. His hair fluffs over his ears, making a ring toward the back, but the top of his head is shiny and reflective. He reminds me of my dad, maybe because his name was also Bruce, but perhaps it's because all semi-bald men remind me of my dad. It's one of my flaws—an inability to make distinctions. If I met a microorganism on the side of the road, I would not know whether to kill it or not. I wouldn't even know how to begin to distinguish between "good" microorganisms and bad, slimy ones. Scientists are good at making distinctions. Writers are good at making generalizations. We metaphor-makers write about a fat, thick tree, green needles, and plump pinecones and hope the reader extrapolates our meaning to be *healthy forest*. A scientist takes samples from that tree and then the next one and then the next one. The scientist doesn't get to "healthy forest" until she's counted all the trees, diagnosed the dirt, measured the girth, palpated the roots. Microorganisms, tend, it turns out, to be more like writers. They'll extrapolate anything, grow anywhere, make a meal out of metaphors of food.

Bruce Rittmann studies microorganisms and how they can do for us what we could do but don't do for ourselves. As chemists and biologists working for Dow Chemical, Dupont, Johnson & Johnson, Merck, the FDA, the USDA, and Monsanto develop new chemicals, Bruce and his team of graduate students and post-docs work to figure out what to do with those chemicals once they've done their job and have been flushed down the drain.

When you think of microorganisms, the idea of them cleaning water seems counter-intuitive. Aren't the people who buy anti-bacterial everything trying to get rid of microorganisms? Aren't microorganisms in the water the thing you're trying to avoid?

It's important, Bruce notes, "that you understand that the environment under which some microorganisms are helpful and the environment under which some microorganisms do damage. It changes everything. Same is true of pollutants, of course. Some microbes, in some instances, are dangerous. Different microbes, in the same place, do good."

Bruce studies place as much as he studies slime. There are so many microorganisms that most of them aren't even named. But, Bruce clarifies, we don't necessarily need to know each one, individually. We're trying to get to know the microorganisms discretely enough that we can know in what instances some microorganisms can do. We're creating the opportunity for the microorganisms, whoever they are, to do some good work by giving them a place and a circumstance in which to do it.

Bruce says, "The basic science is to create an environment for the useful microorganisms to thrive." He tells his students to "Grab the low hanging fruit" or even better, to keep their eyes open for "falling off the log technology," which means looking for opportunities to find obvious solutions, looking for no-brainer moments. "Not fighting nature but working with nature—follow the pattern of nature, work with natural tendencies and ecosystems." Although scientists rely on singularity in the labs, in this case, a little artistic generalization happens when they apply the science to the scene.

Convincing microorganisms to help humans out is old science. The idea of aerating wastewater for some microbes to "reduce" and oxidize contaminants[1] is as ancient as the Romans. It is also old science to then cap the waste and let the anaerobic microbes take over. Aerobic and then anaerobic microbes. The Romans didn't quite know that there were tiny creatures making dirty water clean again but they knew that exposing sewage-rife water to oxygen for a given amount of time and next, shutting off all oxygen to the sewage, transformed their water back into something potable and not-bad-microorganism-ridden.

All water on earth is treated to a similar process—naturally filtered by sands, through evaporation, in the stomach juices of an oyster. There's only one water. We are all, in effect, drinking dinosaur pee. But what Bruce does takes cleaning this water aerobically and anaerobically to the next level. Those things like nitrates and the Superfund site contaminants like rocket fuel and dry cleaning fluids? Bruce has found microbes that can reduce these contaminants.

Bruce's process is simple. He follows the principle, what does nature *do* in nature? And then he extends the metaphor. The first question he asks is what is a particular microorganism's physiology and metabolism?

"To get a bit anthropomorphic—what motivates a microbe? All organisms work the same. Humans, at the high end of the food chain, need to eat a lot of highly caloric, high-energy food to make the complex systems work. To get the max energy out of them. Microorganisms are at the low end—they can exploit the tiniest bit of energy. Methane for instance. A microorganism just needs a little to be encouraged to respire, eat, reproduce." The microorganism *methylbakter tundripaludum* uses methane to build new cell material and to produce energy and has been used to oxidize methane in landfills and soil. There's hope though that as the climate warms, the bacteria will help compensate by growing and consuming more methane. But it needs oxygen to work and, if global warming persists and permafrost melts, the bacteria might drown. Then the work they do to reduce global warming will be, thanks to global warming, put to an end.

I asked about microorganisms reducing the oil plume in the gulf. What were they doing before all that oil burst forth from BP's pipeline? He explains that oil has always been seeping from the ocean floor. Now there was just more of it. To the microbes on the ocean floor, oil is regular food. (The food metaphor seeps in—even with Bruce. Scientists like metaphors too). But when more of it poured out, when the pipeline cut loose from the ocean floor. It was like they were being served doughnuts. Too many oil-eating microbes may be bad for the ecosystem just like too many doughnuts may be bad for the human digestive system. Bruce says the protozoa will eat the microbes and so on and so on. Changing the ecology but not necessarily ruining it. Hopefully. It could go bad. They microorganisms, as they multiply, could denude the ocean of oxygen, or make it overly acidic, or affect the protozoa, then the protozoa-eating fish, then the fish-eating fish, then the bird-eating birds, then the bird-eating alligators with oil-eating microbes which may or may not be a good diet for the fish, birds, or alligators. Like butter or chocolate or bacon, even good things can be too much of a good thing.

A senior advisor at the White House called Bruce during the Gulf Oil spill for some science advice. People were trying to sell the government microorganisms to pour into the ocean. He told the advisor it was probably a bad idea for two reasons—one, you'd need so many and two, that by the time whoever was selling could grow them, they will have naturally grown themselves. He thought it looked like a good way for microorganism-researchers to make a quick government buck.

"It's important to remember that some microbes naturally do this work," Bruce said. Some microorganisms abound or lay low depending on the circumstances, for instance, a BP refinery explosion that, in turn, makes their population explode. Finding the right microorganism, Bruce said, isn't usually that hard. There's usually more than one that will do the trick. That's why they don't have to name each of the individually.

Maggie's Farm, Farmville, USA

Microorganisms reduce nitrates found in crop fertilizer. Bruce has found several microbes that, if introduced to a nitrate-rich environment, will begin to exchange that nitrate for food, reducing the nitrate in the drinking water.

Nitrate, NO_3 comes from fertilizer. Fertilizer runs off agricultural fields into the neighboring ground water, into the neighboring rivers. By the time the fertilizer makes it back downtown to the water treatment plant, the water, in the form of run-off, in the form of rivers, in the form of sewers, in the form of storm drain, has carried past home and home and home. Now that the suburbs have become exurbs, farmland and homestead are neighbors once again like they were in the idyllic agricultural past when houses and farms abutted, although now in a much more Costco-sized manner. Big houses. Big, agricultural fields. Big fertilizers.

Fertilizer isn't any newer than the home-farm connection. Humans have been using organic compounds to feed their plants since the beginning of gardening. If you have a choice between planting a seed in black, rich, manure-rich humus or in sandy, gray, flat, dirt, the black soil is the obvious choice. What's not so natural are synthetic fertilizers. These are made from a combination of ammonia and urea which provide all kinds of macronutritents—primarily, nitrogen, phosphorus and potassium, and secondarily, calcium, sulfur and magnesium—and some micronutrients—in this case, the trace minerals boron, chlorine, manganese, iron, zinc, copper, molybdenum, and selenium.

Without the inorganic and synthetic fertilizers developed in the past 150 years, the population would probably be half what it is today. Population explosion, awesome or awful, is nevertheless filled with awe. Thanks to the development of nitrates produced on an industrial scale, nitrate-fertilized crops support half the world's population through its extreme chemical maneuvers. Sprinkle it on lettuce, tomatoes, cabbage and watch your vegetables grow and grow and grow.

That big, booming carrot in your vegetable crisper would be a tiny little thing without artificial nitrates. It also probably took a barrel of oil to grow that carrot as big as it is. Organic carrots are spindly and curvy and not as bright orange. Chemical manipulation helps to sculpt wayward-growing carrots into perfect, Bugs Bunny-seducing, supermarket carrots. Once, I took a carrot from the farmer's market to my grandmother when she was living in an assisted-living apartment, with its one-bedroom attempt to look like it wasn't adjacent a nursing home, but with the nursing home smell percolating over the transom and under the door. (Please note the gas-guzzling I myself did, driving to the farmer's market, driving back to my mother's. The farmer's drove their trucks from their farms to the square. It is not an entirely guilt-free carrot.) The dirt from the bunch of carrots put a dent in that smell. And although her hips were no longer her own, her teeth were. She bit that carrot like she wasn't going to die within the month. She bit that carrot like she remembered pulling them from her backyard garden. She said she hadn't tasted a carrot like that since my dad was a kid.

But no one lives by carrots alone, even big, bulky, synthetically fertilized carrots. The crops that are propping up the global populace are wheat and corn and rice. And when you've got so many crops to feed and such a record population to grow, you don't skimp on the good stuff. The farmers use enough nitrates to grow an extra planet. And the nitrogen that the Bugs Bunny-worthy carrot, or wheat, or corn, can't absorb is left behind on the fields.

In the west, nitrate stays behind on the fields in dry form, at least until the monsoons. When the rains come, the nitrate that has been sitting on top of the soil, on top of the neighboring crops, on top of the crops that have yet to be harvested, is flushed. Flushing implies a cleansing but like all cleansings, the water has to go somewhere. The rain takes the nitrates into the streams that contribute to the rivers that flow to the Colorado, that, on good years, flow into the Pacific Ocean. Some of the nitrates, on their way down the Rocky Mountains and under and across the deserts are left behind, changing the cornflowers, the sage, and the chaparral in the coastal forests. The animals eat the nitrates too in high altitude lakes in Estes Park Rocky Mountain National Park, in Lake Tahoe, in Mirror Lake in the Uintahs in Utah. The deer drink from those pristine-looking lakes. The fish swim in them. Owls dive-bomb the fish. The nitrates, like the PFOAs, persist in the most tucked-in folds of the wilderness.

Along the way to the ocean, the nitrates seep into ground water. They end up in wastewater treatment plants. They end up back in the drinking water—you might taste them, if you're highly sensitive to the flavor of ammonia. You might gravitate toward them if you like a clean tongue and hope to one day adapt toward photosynthetic capabilities.

Nitrogen balance is tricky. Nitrogen in soil is good but too much is bad. Nitrates in your food may be unhealthy. Too much nitrate in your blood is bad, especially for babies. If they get too much nitrate in their system, the nitrate is converted to nitrite in the infant's gut, a place where it inhibits the baby's growth. Some research has suggested that when the nitrite combines with hemoglobin, it forms methemoglobin, limiting bloods ability to carry oxygen. They call it blue baby syndrome. Most babies need as much oxygen as their blood can get them, especially prematurely born infants who are prone to other cyanotic diseases like respiratory distress syndrome. In fact, too much nitrate in the water can make a regular-term baby act like a premature one, requiring doctors to keep the baby in the hospital and deliver oxygen nasally. Sometimes these babies require transfusions. Methemoglobinemia can easily be treated with supplemental oxygen. But, if you're living in the world of too many nitrates in the water, treating the symptoms isn't really a cure.

North Dakota by Fall

It's not that the farmer wants your baby to turn blue. The farmer doesn't even know where his carrots are at the moment. Or his wheat. Or his corn. He no longer stands on the porch of his farmhouse and look over his crops. He no longer digs his hand into the dirt or breaks his knuckles on rock to see if this is the exact right consistency for fertility. His grandfather could weigh the amount of nitrate and phosphate and potassium by the heaviness of the dirt in his hand, in the way a granule turned upside down reveals its mineral content. By smelling it, he knew if there was a good amount of copper, selenium, iron and zinc. It's not that his senses equaled the precision of a mass spectrometer. It's more that he knew what the ground was supposed to feel and smell like. He put some in his mouth to taste its balance.

To grow crops plentiful enough to feed not the hundreds but the billions, you would need millions of farmers to go into the fields and taste the dirt. There are not that many farmers. No one has walked on the fields where they grow these things in a long time. A company of threshers starts the harvest in mid-May and works its way up by tractor to North Dakota by fall. The semis drive their tractors from large farm to large farm. The men climb from truck to thresher. The threshers spin across the fields, in mile-wide formations, cutting across fields as easily as a man shaves across his cheek. The only difference the tractor-drivers note is that their coffee at Dunkin Donuts tastes sweeter below the Mason-Dixon line, that there are more Starbucks on the coast, that Tim Horton coffee rules the north and northeast.

The nitrates mostly come and go through our bodies with no absolute effect on our health—cancer predictions haven't been substantiated—but they don't just reside in our bodies. Like everything else, they're flushed back into the world, down the drain, into the sewer, to the wastewater treatment center where they go back into the rivers, into the ground water, toward the ocean where they do more effective harm to fish than they do to people. And then the people eat the fish and the oceans rain the rain and the story abounds and resounds and accumulates and accumulates in the soil, in the water, in your baby, in your fish, in your flesh.

The air wants its nitrogen back.

Dr. Bruce Rittmann honors the air's request. His metaphor of grabbing-the-low-hanging-fruit, of falling-off-the-log logic, of just follow nature's true course pays off. It's not, usually, a matter of finding the one right microorganism—there are many good ones and they're hard, even for his discerning genius, to tell apart. It's when he introduces microorganisms from one environment into another that the magic happens. A wide-variety of microorganisms are able to transform nitrate. They just happened to live somewhere else and ate whatever conveniently surrounded them. The microorganisms didn't even know they *liked* nitrate. But Dr. Rittman, by giving them an opportunity to try it, finds out they do. With little effort on their part, they turn nitrate to nitrogen gas. Microorganisms are low-overhead. Bruce contrasts them to humans. "People like nice wine. Some of them will buy a three-hundred-dollar bottle because they like it. They think it tastes good. They think it's worth it. But microorganisms don't care. They'll drink your three-hundred-dollar bottle but, just as easily, they'll drink boxed wine. They'll drink malt liquor. They are not too particular as long as you give them something to eat." Microbiologists and writers seem to share a love of metaphor. And wine.

Just like those oil-eating microbes used the oil as sustenance and converted it to something less toxic so did these microbes reduce, in the chemical sense of give electrons to as well as to reduce the contamination itself, the nitrate in the soil. These just needed to be persuaded to the deliciousness that is nitrate. They not only like the taste, they need it. Even if you've grown to like nitrate-tasting carrots, your body can't do anything with that extra nitrate. The microorganisms can.

At the Cleaners

Dry cleaners used to clean clothes using trichloroethylene (TCE). Although TCEs were phased out in the fifties, they were an amazing solvent, dissolving grass stains and blood stains and all kinds of slime stains away. But TCEs contaminated soil, so that when it rained, much like the nitrate, TCE leeched into ground water. A good percentage of it resolved in the air, meaning it rained down again. But even though TCEs were replaced by PCE, tetrachloroethylene, the bad news is abundant. One highlight, from the EPA website, reads, "Effects resulting from acute, inhalation exposure of humans to tetrachloroethylene vapors include irritation of the upper respiratory tract and eyes, kidney dysfunction, and at lower concentrations, neurological effects, such as reversible mood and behavioral changes, impairment of coordination, dizziness, headache, sleepiness, and unconsciousness."

This is acute, meaning direct, contact. But studies have also shown that there are severe reproductive and developmental effects that include spontaneous abortion, menstrual disorders, altered sperm structure, birth defects and fetal resorption of tetrachloroethylene with casual contact.

A woman I know married a man who ran a drycleaner. After her seventh miscarriage—each in the fourth month—just at the time when she was getting used to the pregnancy, just when she was almost convinced that fetus might stick around this time, just when she started wondering, is this body growing on its own? She gave up trying to stay pregnant. Whatever forces were conspiring for the fetus to grow met head-on with forces that prescribed the ways of water. Gravity happens. Gravity, with a little added PCE, is a force she had to learn to live with. Once upon a time, maybe, her body, its inertia, its biological drive toward new life, could have resisted gravity. But now, gravity colluded with more target-specific forces.

There's no certain way to blame the PCEs for her miscarriages. For all we know it could have been PCEs in the water or any string of chemical compounds, or, of course, nothing chemically induced at all. Although scientists working with Bruce are currently compiling the database to correlate Superfund neighborhoods with numbers of hospital visits, correlation isn't the same as cause and effect. There are enough unnatural entities in the water to blame the water generally, not the PCEs or TCEs specifically. There are enough unnatural entities in the air to blame the air. When you're so pregnant-tender that you can't even wear a tight shirt for the pressure it exerts against your breasts, it feels natural. When you are eating a saltine cracker as you lie in bed too nauseated to get up, that feels natural. When you fall asleep, head on the kitchen table, right after lunch, waking up with sandwich bread stuck to your forehead, that feels natural.

What feels unnatural is the unraveling of your belly button, the tug of an ovary, the stitch in your side that you weren't supposed to feel again for nine months. It's easy to blame unnatural forces for miscarriages. Spiteful, naked, you sit on the bare dirt, bleed into it, and give back to the earth the bad dirt it gave to you. Maybe it was the dry-cleaning detergent. Maybe it was the rocket fuel. Maybe it was a natural unwinding to an inevitable unwound ending. But, if you get pregnant next time, you filter your water. You hope there are some of those TCE-oxiding microorganisms thriving naturally in the ground water outside your house. You hope they find a PCE-adapting microorganism. You adapt a little yourself. You make your dry-cleaning husband wash his clothes in regular laundry detergent before he comes to bed. It's more of a superstition than a remedy, but you would like to pretend you have a little control over the territory of your body.

Rocket fuel and semi-conductor production have left perchlorates all over the southwest like an invasive species. At Superfund sites, Bruce and his teams of graduate students have released several key microorganisms to reduce the level of contamination. These microorganisms do the hard work the forest rangers do, but on a chemical, rather than physical level. The ranger pulls at an invasive Tamarisk tree. The roots have locked themselves deeply into the southwestern rivers banks. The ranger's hands are raw, her arms ache, but she is ebullient, effervescent with her accomplishment. Tamarisk produce a million seeds a year. They steal the water from the indigenous plants. They crowd out the natural flora, thereby killing the native flora. Tamarisk are a macro problem. It's easy to be ecstatic when stuffing one into the coffin of a plastic bag. The microorganisms know that ebullience if not that ecstasy. They throw their electrons off onto those invasive perchlorates. They dig their ecological mission, if only because it makes them light and airy and bubbly as club soda.

Finding microorganisms that love living in the places where perchlorates and nitrates flourished was relatively easy for Bruce. Microorganisms exist in all kinds of places: in ponds, in the dirt, on the edges of pine needles, on your eyelashes, at the bottom of the ocean, in the extremely briny water of the Great Salt Lake where they're called extremophiles. Microorganisms from all over the place, so many different species of microbes, love the taste of nitrate and perchlorates.

But tetrachlorethylene, the dry-cleaning solvent, has no natural microbial partners. When Bruce says, "follow nature's path, do what nature does," that works well for nitrates since there are so many microbes able to help out. But perchlorate is different—only one or two strains within the species were able to do the work. Bruce needed to physically supply the contaminated area with the microbes instead of, as he had done with nitrates, creating a more ideal environment for the organisms.

Is there anything these microorganisms won't do? Answer: yes. See triclosan. Also PFOAs. Also titanium oxide—the teeth whitening agent in your toothpaste. But Bruce is working on finding good microbial partners for them. Until then, I throw out my non-stick pan. I let my scrambled egg pan soak. My teeth. They're a little yellow but my husband doesn't notice. I don't need titanium oxide. I want my gut biome to keep me from getting Crohn's disease but every soap I find has triclosan. So I just stop using soap.

Oasisamerica

Microorganisms: work, reduce, mitigate, eat, resolve, transfer, chemically react, come to the rescue, at least in certain circumstances. Bruce points out, "They do the same things we do." They eat. They excrete. They convert food into a different kind of energy. In the right place, at the right time, they do good work. They also, from the human perspective, do plenty of bad work: cholera and botulism, just to name a few human-destroying microorganisms. The concept of good and bad is, of course, a human one. The microorganisms are just doing their thing, eating, reproducing, respiring.

Between the 7th and 14th centuries, the Hohokam built a system of canals between the lower Salt River and the middle Gila River to irrigate what is now known as the Phoenix basin. This irrigation system rivaled in complexity those built in ancient China, Egypt, and the near East. People have been organizing and reforming water for centuries, for better or for worse. Now, one additional problem we have, toxins in our water, has a potential, if partial, solution. The microorganism, borrowed from another scene, returns that perc-ridden water to Hohokam-fresh water.

This is a good thing for the microorganisms to do for humans. It is a natural thing for microorganisms. The ideas of good or bad don't trouble the microbe. It is bad thing when botulism bacteria colonize digestive tract, causing first, the eyelids to droop and flicker, then making it hard for the baby to move his arms, then, in severe cases, making the exchange of carbon dioxide into oxygen in the blood difficult, then impossible. The botulism doesn't think this is a bad idea. Its colonization of the digestive tract is the same as its colonization of fields of nitrate. In fact, even in a field of nitrates, the microorganisms might run amok, over-reproducing and over-colonializing, causing their own kind of damage, like algae blooms that choke the oxygen from reaching plants or fish. But, in a different environment, a little botulinum toxin produced by

Clostridum botuinum can reduce the wrinkles around the eyes. Pressed. Skin. Managed microbes.

The concern of course is that we keep pretending humans have foresight. This microbe helps now. Will it help later? Miles of pens of salmon rattling against Chile's coast, radiation seeping from the Fukushima Daiichi nuclear plant, dumping toxins into well-water, into streams, into oceans, cutting down forests to make paper, to grow cattle for meat, idling our cars in the drive-thru and leaving the lights on all night, making the atmosphere hotter, thawing ice caps, making the polar bears swim.

Microorganisms eating perchlorate are as self-serving as humans cutting down pollution filtering forests to grow cows for meat. Microorganisms do what they do and we do what we do. Microorganisms are happy eating and respiring whether inside a dented tin can or a seep of perchlorate. We enjoy our carrots fat whether we're next to the farm or in the North Pole.

We are, as far as the planet is concerned, microorganisms—we harm the planet, we fix the planet, we do and undo. Microorganisms, like people, are persuadable. Microorganisms are adapters, fixers, heroes, destroyers, builders, recyclers, breathers, eaters, reproducers. They adapt to the environment. They adapt the environment to suit them. They have the capacity to change the chemical make-up of the planet.

But the metaphor between humans and microorganisms breaks down when you think about place. When the microorganism runs out of food, it stops adapting, it stops respiring, reducing toxins or reproducing selves—it slows down. It eats less. It self corrects. There are limits to its ability to create its own environment. Microbes can't get in a car and move to the next delicious Superfund site or to the next dented tin can. Someone, be it a human, an animal, a waterway, or a microbe-transporting breeze, has to take it there.

Humans, self-propelling, if not self-correcting, take themselves everywhere—they bring the carrots, fat and pointed, with them. They plant the carrot seeds in whatever soil they choose. They pump the nitrates into the soil. They hope they discover a microbe that turns their water back into unadulterated toxin-free water.

◎

Notes

1. I would like to call what they do "eat" but no one likes to think of things eating sewage, not even microorganisms. In chemistry, "to reduce" means to add electrons. This is one reason it's hard to translate chemistry. Eat is a metaphor and it's not exactly right although the scientists seem to use "to eat" as shorthand for what the microbes chemically do. Reducing adds electrons, which chemically changes the pollutant from noxious to null. To reduce by adding is counterintuitive but then so is sending slimy things in to

fight even grosser things. As my chemist friend, Gabe, clarifies in a micro-essay of his own, "When I apply the word 'eat' to bacteria, I'm tending to think of the process of extracting energy from food, but of course a broader perspective would appreciate that we're breaking up the food (usually a process during which the food molecules ultimately get oxidized) but then we're building new pieces of ourselves (often a chemical reduction). If your use of the term 'eat' encompasses both, then it'll have to involve both oxidation and reduction. If you rather separate the two ideas, then eat means I burn the food I eat for energy (almost non-metaphorically true, as the chemistry of burning sugar and metabolizing sugar give identical products).

Micromanagement

It was a chewing thing. Chewing up the scenery. Chewing up the fat. Chewing up all the gossip I'd been telling that girl. And, worse, it then turned into a swallowing thing. Peristalsis of the heart. A condition best left to lovers, not women, sitting at their kitchen table, blaming their second cup of coffee for making the heart noticeable. My computer blinked. Maybe this whole house's electrical system has gone bad. Maybe it's not my heart. But then the computer stayed on and my heart blinked aloud again. It should be a silent thing. Quiet. Not dramatic. Not a masticating, starving ham.

I blamed myself. The ham that had been really not ham. I bought the quarter-hog in an attempt to be good. Buy local. No antibiotics. Raised humanely. No nitrates. But let me tell you, a ham with no nitrates, or at least no cure, is no ham at all. It's a fatty leg of pork and now my heart is making a lot of noise about itself.

It snowed that morning. I blame the snow. No one wants it to snow in April any more than they want overcooked pork on Easter. The snowflakes took the apple blossoms down with it and global warming makes it hard to eat locally anyhow. Winter delayed and then fell like a hammer.

I tried to explain to the triage nurse that it felt like my heart was swallowing itself. I could feel the aorta open up and gulp the blood. It felt like a hiccup. She didn't blame me, even when I told her about the cup of coffee, even when I told her about the pain in my ribs I had felt at 2:52 in the morning (pain level: 4) and didn't drive through the snow to the ER right then. I almost told her about the ham but she interrupted me. "It sure is busy today. Usually, when it snows, no one comes in."

"They should stay home," I agreed. I agreed again. I didn't want to be there either.

I was reading Pam Houston's new book about listening more closely when people talk when the nurse with the probes came in, peeled off the back of the adhesive, and hooked me up to the monitors. As if I wasn't electric enough.

"I never have time to read," she said. "My daughter still sleeps with me. She's four."

"I don't know how any of us get any sleep at night. I still sleep by my son." Max was six months old. My heart was too young to go on the blink, wasn't it?

"Ever since my husband moved out, she's just wanted to be close."

I pictured her four-year-old's body taking the place of a man's. How much more room she must have. How much colder the bed must be. I like it cold.

"How does the baby sleep?" I asked.

"Oh, he's doing fine. Hasn't noticed much that my husband has been gone at all."

The metallic detectors did what they needed to, EKG detected me. I was in a spy novel. Then, with new stickers, she hooked me to the regular room monitors and I was no longer in a novel at all.

I blamed myself. It's always the wine. It was red. I pictured the wine scouring my arteries. Cleaning them out like Drano down a sink clogged with bacon fat. But maybe not. Maybe wine gums more than cleans. But let me tell you, you'd have a glass of wine too after teaching a student who kept reminding you he also has a PhD and he thought that story we read for class was as rehashed and rehearsed and as unbelievable as a pile of eggs. "Writing is like cholesterol. It hinges things. Its purpose is to heal bad arteries but too much cholesterol shuts down the system," I said to the class, which cut through the tension but didn't heal anything.

Dawn, a different nurse, came in to draw blood. Her arms were masterpieces. "You work out?" I wasn't hitting on her but I did like her biceps. "I can tell by your arms."
"CrossFit," she said.
I should have known. My good friend does CrossFit and even though I laughed when Dawn said CrossFit, because, well, there's a certain over-the-toppedness there what with the over-unders and the medicine balls, but still, I asked where she went, what the schedule was.

"There's a class at 10, 11, 12, 2, 4, 5 and I think 6." CrossFitters are good proselytizers.

"Maybe it's good for your heart," I said.

She said, "It's good for everything."

When the doctor came in and said, "I don't think you're having a heart attack," I reached over for my phone even though the sign said, "no cell phone use behind this door." A text is not a cell and I had to tell someone I was getting out of there.

I neglected to mention the feeling of little tiny hands grasping the bottom of my rib cage. But he didn't ask and the monitors didn't tell and the nurse was giving me advice on how to catch the medicine ball for the first time. I had my shirt back on by the time he said, "Has work been particularly difficult lately?" There is, I know, no cure for life.

Sometimes, when I cough, the gurgling sensation stops. Sometimes, when I drink a glass of wine it stops. It never stops with coffee and although I went running on Wednesday, Friday, and Monday, I could not tell if my heart was hurting or if my neck was aching or if this is always how I feel when I run and therefore why I run so slowly, so briefly. Maybe my heart has been bad since the get-go and I am just finally learning that this is how a hungry heart sounds.

◎

Micronize

I used to believe that if you wanted something, it was sure to come. Sure enough, Christmas and birthdays came every year. And then I grew up and went swimming a lot, enough that I realized I had a body and other people had bodies and that swimming with other bodies meant that someone wanted to swim in my body but not necessarily with my body. I wanted to be a dolphin. I believed. I never became. So then I believed the opposite—that thing my mom used to say, "you'll never find love it you go looking for it" —so I kept my eyes on the ground and didn't look at anyone and stopped swimming entirely. Then I believed in mind over matter again because I'd read Adorno and though I wanted to fight it I couldn't. Poetry was over because no one believed that anything small and beautiful could happen if something so big and awful had happened. That poetry was the art of wonder and no one wondered anymore. Everyone had been vaporized and there was no mystery to that. But then I believed, once, when I was digging up worms to move to my herb garden, that perhaps the mind didn't matter. That perhaps matter made its own course. And the wind, vapor as it was, small particles of matter beating against my body, turned my hair this way so I turned my head that way, and that was wonderful in its dark and faithless way. I could believe in worms. They have bodies. Which is at least something solid to believe in.

◎

Microhabitat

A tree, fallen in the forest, turns to hair. What is the purpose of hair? To keep germs out of the nose. To keep grains of sand out of the eyes. To keep the head warm when the snow piles on, when the winter begins to think everything is dead and ready to be reinvested, recycled, reincarnated in the dirt. But not everything is dead on the hair. Dust mites, even on the dead, still clean the eyelashes. The nasal cilia cling to the inside of the nose. The roots of cold hair turn colder under snow.

The tree, though fallen, isn't dead. I have seen, on the hairs of the decomposing tree, a banana slug the length of my arm scratching its underbelly against grain. In its slimy path, a microbe nestles. It is fed by the slime. It respires the hairs of the fallen the tree, turning the hair to humus, opening the chemical strand to let new carbon in. Deep inside the fallen tree, under the hair, the carbon cycles. It looks for its rhizome partner. The rhizome has been waiting for this little death for 223 years. Tickled by the carbon, the rhizome swells, breaks through stiff hair. The mushroom rises up, engorged. Its spores search for wind. The wind, carrying spores and oxygen to vie for space with all this decomposing carbon, brings its own reformation. It streams through the hairs, parting them, opening space for the seed from the pinecone to lodge. Inside its old tree, under the warmth of a tropical slug, beside a lascivious rhizome, surrounded by the microbe-pulsing humus, the seed of the Douglas Fir stretches out its cilia in the skeleton of forest. Its sprout clings to a tendril of hair. The hair hoists the sprout. The sprout. The first hair. The next tree.

◎

Neutrinos

When I was fifteen, I read a book about a mute girl who went to a bar to see a show. She went into the bathroom and came out with the lead singer's name carved into her forehead. The lead singer, guilty and guilted, married the girl. It wasn't until after the wedding, after the baby, after years of silence, that the lead singer, who doesn't sing anymore, discovers it was not his wife who cut his name in her forehead. A stranger accosted his now-wife in the bathroom and carved his name in her forehead. Should he have married that woman instead?

Neutrinos could tell us but neutrinos, in their mathematic existence, don't talk. If the universe is indeed expanding, then we will surely never die. Of course, we get the news too late. Dead stars sending obituaries of light. The name reads backwards in the mirror. We can't see our future until it's very well past.

I Googled this: "Cesar girl carved name bathroom singer." Google came back with a different book, one by Anne Tyler about a different girl who carved the name of a singer she had a crush on into her forehead. It is not the same book. My book had a woodcut of the word "Cesar" on the cover. But Google thought it already knew what I was going to ask.

It is very difficult to observe neutrinos, especially muon and tau neutrinos. First you must know neutrons, electrons and protons. Then you must know anti-neutrinos. You must invite them over for video games. Once you have gotten to know them, they try to steal the joy stick. The way the hand goes slack. The speed of resignation. You now have all the control in your hands. And now you know something else about the universe. Neutrinos are weak.

The book, not my book but Anne Tyler's, is now a movie starring Guy Pearce. I can't picture Guy Pearce but I think of Pierce Brosnan who played Remington Steele about the same time as I read my book about the girl who carved/was carved with the name of her future husband that she did not necessarily already love.

There are so many neutrinos in the universe that even a small neutrino mass can display great significance. Think of the Grand Canyon. Think of a piece of sand. Think of a piece of sand falling into the Grand Canyon, into the river. Weigh the Colorado. How do you measure absence? What did moving that grain of sand dislodge? How did it lose itself in its fall? "The energy spectrum of the observable electrons in a radioactive beta decay is modified if the electron neutrino has a non-zero mass. The unseen neutrinos are emitted uniformly in momentum, but for a massive neutrino the change in energy for momenta up to about 0.5^*m^*c is small, so a relatively large number of electrons are emitted at close to the maximum energy."[1] It was bad enough when we were asked to imagine light speed and stars signaling light back to us that had so long ago gone out. How do you measure the dark cut, the cave, the cut-out? Non-zero mass. Unseen neutrinos. A plummet into a future that might have already disappeared.

In another bar, in Salt Lake, then called The Fat Squirrel or the Urban Lounge or "across from the Greek place" in another bathroom with stalls with no doors at all, let alone locks, I was accosted by a woman whose husband was a musician. His name was not carved into her forehead so you couldn't exactly call it love but she told me to marry my musician, she held my arms behind my back, marched me to the toilet. That is where love is. She flushed and flushed until I forgot about my old boyfriend, the neutrino one, whose lock on his truck door was broken. She pushed me out the door into the boyfriend who was like her husband in that the music swallowed him, in that his dancing was limited to one foot tapping, in that at night, on the red vinyl of his GMC pickup I could see myself in his mirror and even though I didn't carve the word "Cesar" into my forehead, I did cut my name into the bench seat of that truck of that forward moving truck. There was no going back.

The Sudbury Neutrino Observatory (SNO), once fully operational, will be able to detect all three types of neutrinos, and if we are lucky enough to have a nearby supernova, the SNO may be able to improve the limits on the muon and tau neutrinos. But the supernova has already happened and the measuring has already begun. The universe is heavier, more written, more full of that black inky stuff you call sky more full of blood and forehead more full of bathroom stalls and locks and knives and edges than the most powerful telescope, more red and piercing than Hubble can measure.

Eleven years later, that scar on the bench seat still cuts into my leg when we go four-wheeling off Highway 180 taking the back roads to the Grand Canyon. We have expanded, not just fat ways and not just children ways, but in we scribbled our names over and over ways, over the top of each other until the words we were writing became something more than light. Heavy now, not better, not worse, but as invisible and massive as any neutrino and as already always there, staving off death even as the truck barrels faster down that already-rutted road.

Notes

1. Wright, Edward, L. "Neutrinos as Dark Matter," <http://www.astro.ucla.edu/~wright/neutrinos.html>

Microwine

All this global warming and I can't find a decent bottle of Rosé.
—Gabrielle Calvocoressi

I do not come from a family of Italians who drink wine. I do not come from a family of French who drink wine. I come from a family of Utahns who drink wine, which made my family somewhat outcast in Utah. It also means my knowledge of wine is not inherited from the soil. As with all white people in Utah, my love of wine is immigrant. It's as imported into my blood as the wine my parents drank—which was not wine from either Italy or France and definitely not from Utah but from California where they make big boxes of wine. My understanding of wine came from assumption, soap operas, and marketing.

Reunite on ice. Chardonnay on ice. Chardonnay out of a box. Light. Golden. Perfectly Californian. Dreams get wrapped up in that. Weddings in the vineyard. Toasting on the beach. A deck over the crashing ocean, glass of wine in hand, green to the back of me, a fantasy of blue to the front. And golden chardonnay in my glass. Golden hair tumbling down my back. Everyone wants California. Chardonnay. California in a cup.

When I started working at the Oregon Winegrowers I learned this: The first rule of a good wine? Let it be red. Of the sips of wine I'd taken from my parents' cold glasses, Chardonnay tastes like salad dressing filtered through burnt walnut shells. But pinot noir. That tasted like cherry blossoms in winter. And so it began. A new dream. No wedding. Instead, I would buy a winery myself. I would have great big parties in my vineyard in McMinnville on tables lined with wine and salmon. During harvest, we'd have an old-time grape-stomping party. Off with your shoes. My children would run through the vines. *The Wine Spectator* would visit. Take pictures of my wine, sun filtering through the glass, stained with red, still letting sun through.

Except we're in Oregon. There is too little sun on this side of the Cascades to grow the full-bodied wine I want to grow. There is also no million dollars to buy this vineyard or that winery. *Wine Spectator* must have lost my phone number. They never showed up to rate my wine that I never made. There were no children. I adapted my dreams. I moved on from the Oregon Winegrowers to the Oregon Humane Society. If I couldn't have a lot of wine and vines, at least I could have a lot of cats.

Growing up in Salt Lake, I didn't know I lived in a desert. Having been born there, arid mountains and brown summer grass were normal. But when I came back from Portland, where even the asphalt turns green, layered with a crop of moss, cracking drought covered everything. Even what looked like soft green grass snapped in bony half when you pulled a blade from the ground. I put fliers on my neighbors' lawns suggesting they try xeriscaping or at least stop watering the sidewalk. I collected rainwater to water my garden even though it is illegal to do so in Utah, because in Utah someone downstream owns the water rights to that falling rain. I felt smug in my rebellion. I sat on the back patio drinking wine imported from California. I felt guilty for the fossil fuels that brought me my drink but I felt confirmed in my smugness knowing I was drinking someone else's water right.

It's a cliché to say that you worry about the planet for your kids. But it was true. I pictured a planet turned from an Oregon into a Utah. Where would the children play if not between rows of green vines? Where would they dream of getting married? How would they celebrate without wine?

I have no winery but I do, finally, have some children. My son, Max, likes wine already. He is three and when I finish a glass, he is allowed to take the last sip, which is really no sip at all but it's enough to tickle his tongue. I hope I'm not subjecting him to a lifelong problem with alcohol. And I certainly hope I'm not coloring his palate with red wine so that when he grows up, he rebels and drinks white. For now, he is content with the droplet of wine. He is outside playing in the dirt because we have no grass. We live in Flagstaff, Arizona now. It's as dry as Utah, except we get monsoons. The green that we have here is not bottom-up green like they have in Oregon. It's top-down green with the branches of the Ponderosa. I'll take it. If the Ponderosa will. I heard somewhere that if these trees burn down or otherwise die, new Ponderosa won't take their place. The monsoons are too short now. The snowpack too shallow. Something will take their place. Maybe even something green. But it won't be vines. And it won't be grass.

Max stumbles over one of the solidified lava rocks in the front yard. I set down my wineglass and run to him. A rock has split open the skin on his forehead. He's OK but what I would give for a lawn that yields to falling foreheads. In Salt Lake, I thought grass was such a sin but now that I have kids, I have changed my mind. I would like to be better but the more kids I have, the longer I don't live in Portland, the more I drive. My friend Misty still lives in Portland. She tows her five-year-old daughter to school in a trailer attached to her bike. She locks up the trailer and then rides on to work. I have two kids. I have become so the opposite of Portland-good.

The winegrowers are trying to be optimistic about climate change. It's worth a try, I think. Why spend your days imagining whole forests turned to desert? Whole ice caps melted? Whole polar bears drowning? Humans are basically optimists and people who grow grapes are good at looking at the bright side of things. In Canada, thanks to global warming, vintners are already hoping they will be able to raise cabernet sauvignon grapes. You cannot grow cabernet grapes in Canada, was the old belief. The season is too short for cabernet grapes which require a long, warm growing season. Pinot noir, a cool-air loving grape, does well there.

The winegrowers are thinking across several levels of adaptation, from the variations that will happen outdoors to what they can do indoors in the winery to adjust their practices to compensate for these changing fruits. "One is what can we do in the vineyard to adapt to what looks to be very variable and very challenging weather," says research scientist Gary Pickering. "The second general approach is what can we do in the winery in terms of adapting to changing the juice composition that we may start to see." The vintners are good at something I am not: staying in place to adapt to change. I keep moving like I can stay ahead of the changes I cannot control—like global warming or drought or bad politics or bad drivers. I vow to leave Arizona if they keep cutting the education budget. I vow to leave if these Californians don't stop cutting me off in traffic. But where will I move? California? Where I can grow cabernet? Where the politics aren't so bad but the water situation is equally dire.

The winegrowers fight other aspects of natures too. Phylloxera, almost microscopic, pale yellow sap-sucking, aphid-like insects that feed on the roots and leaves of grapevines, destroyed over half the grape vines in Europe in the 19th century. Thereafter, vintners combated the problem by grafting well-known grape varietals like cabernet sauvignon to relatively unknown rootstock from the United States. Because phylloxera is native to the Americas, that rootstock has inherent resistance. But now stubby toe and pin nematodes, roundworms that eat at the roots of vines, have become increasingly difficult to deal with because rootstock resistant to phylloxera isn't resistant to nematodes. Nematodes withstand even with synthesized chemicals. Winegrowers, especially small producers, prefer a non-chemical solution anyway. To adapt their fields to the nematode onslaught, viticulturists plant mustard, which repels the nematodes. Sulfur for mildew, fans to circulate air to prevent vine rot, tents pitched over vines to keep the frost from turning the grapes to otter pops, and a willingness to pull up merlot vines and substitute pinot noir after the merlot-snubbing movie *Sideways*—winegrowers use natural resources, technology, and pure stubbornness to induce their plants adapt to change and simultaneously change their own ways to accommodate the equally-stubborn willfulness of the plants.

I adapted once. I used to drink beer. In Portland, even when I worked at the Winegrowers', I drank more beer than wine. As much as Oregon would like to be wine country, Portland proper is beer land. IPAs and reds, ryes and pales, wheats and porters. Beer beer beer everywhere. Twenty-ounce pints at The Horse Brass with Andy. We broke up there. Nick and I made out in the parking lot and then never saw each other again. Jonathan and I talked about not getting married at the long table in the corner. Two twenty-ounce pints add up. Maybe the beer was driving the men away.

When I moved to Salt Lake, I switched to wine. And then I got married.

Solution solved, as my husband, Erik, would say.

Maybe a man dreams of marrying a woman who drinks less than him ounce by ounce even though he knows she's keeping up drink by drink.

When I worked at the Oregon Winegrowers Association, I had been an English major, not an oenologist. But I could type and I could put a sentence or two together about how the wine grapes in Oregon grew at the 45th parallel—just like Burgundy, France. Metaphors. I could make them. Truly, that band of latitude was the only similarity to which we laid claim. The smaller details like microorganisms in the soil, the amount of limestone and volcano in the soil, the winds, the truly micro-matters did not make it into our publications. We liked to talk about how the plants behaved similarly (no, identically!) to the famous Burgundy grapes of France, where grapes have been adapted to make wine for centuries. The problem with metaphor is, sometimes, that micro-matters matter. That's the point of wine. *Terroir*. You can taste the microorganisms. You can taste the blood of the Celts. That of the Saxons. Of the Vikings. Of the Chumash tribes. The vineyards adapted to the soil as the victors adapted to their newfound home. Easily and with short memories. This soil was always theirs, says the history. Says the metaphor.

~

There's evidence that humans have been growing grapes since the beginning of time. Or at least since 3200 BC. Thucydides writes, "The people of the Mediterranean began to emerge from barbarism when they learnt to cultivate the olive and the vine." Wine is the opposite of barbarism. Wherever humans have adapted to live, grapes seem to follow. From the Republic of Georgia, to the near east, to Germany and France, to Canada, people have figured out what type of grape can grow where and they plant it. Optimists. Although climate change does not bode well right now for grapes grown in Bordeaux or for cold-loving grapes at all. Pinot noir likes a cool climate. Cool is far away. Maybe there will be no cool. But the Canadians persist. We'll move the ice wine vines farther north. Make way for long, dry summers. And, as it warms and dries up in Arizona, cool, wet, Canada is looking better to me every day. Perhaps I can pack up my desert plants and move north too.

My daughter Zoe wants to move north, too, but to Salt Lake where her cousins live. She thinks it's stupid we live far away from our family. "It's my dream to live with Lily." Lily is her cousin who is the same age as Zoe. She tells me this at least twice a week, usually when I'm driving and swearing at traffic, even though compared to real cities, there is no traffic in Flagstaff.

"It is my dream that I have a job so I can feed you and your brother." But this is not really my dream. If I can't have a winery on a river, then my next choice is to have wine with my mom and sisters in Salt Lake City. I am with Zoe on what Flagstaff lacks: a river, a winery, sisters, my mom.

Zoe uses the dreams in the present tense, "I am eating an ice cream cone with caramel sauce. It is my dream," and even in the past tense, "When we are in Disneyland, Lily and I go-ed on a roller coaster that got you all wet. Cameron and Valerie don't want to go because they would get all wet, but Lily and I don't care. We are all wet. Even our underwear. But then it is so hot, we are dry in like five seconds. It is my dream." To Zoe, dreams are ongoing facts. Perhaps that is innocence— the understanding that you're already you're living your dream. My job is to crush her, a little, like a basil leaf, tell her she'll get used to living away from her cousin. It is the hardest part of being a parent, feeding them bad news by the spoonful, inoculating them against worse news later on.

Even though Zoe's dream is to live in Salt Lake, we are all beginning to understand that we actually live here, in Arizona. Flagstaff is good. We live within driving distance of nine national parks and monuments. If we are cold in the winter, we can drive two hours south and find swimming suit weather. If we get too hot in Phoenix, we can gather our jackets and drive north. We are adapting to this variable place. There are people who sought this state out, who chose these varied climates on purpose. Even wine people. There's a guy, Eric Glomski, who grows wine grapes in Arizona on purpose. Although he was born in Chicago, Arizona is his true home. After college at Prescott, he looked for a way to stay in Arizona and found it by buying Page Springs Winery. He makes wine with Maynard Nixon, lead singer of the band Tool. They sell their wine at fancy restaurants in Phoenix. Eric may be my hero. He also may be my fool. He thinks Arizona, as a whole, is great. I want to learn why he chose to grow grapes in one of the weirdest climates in the world.

Adaptation is a strange thing. The verb "to adapt" suggests that it's the thing that can move—the tree's, the agent's, the human's, the bear's job is to change according to its circumstances, as in, there is a tsunami coming toward me so I should move out of the way. Evolution assumes that species adapt to the world, not the other way around. But we humans don't only move to where the water is—we bring it to us. You'd think humans would see that climate change requires changing their ways, to become adapted. But humans are humans. We most often use the verb as transitive. We adapt things to meet our needs. Plant plants that I like to eat and drink. I move this plant and that plant and the wine tastes better now. And meanwhile, geo-engineers strive to find ways to control the climate.

It is summer. School is out and I have the kids. We live in the west, so we are, as always, in the car. On our way down to Page Springs, Max and Zoe sing the four songs we know all the words to. "Mockingbird,"

"Frog Went a Courtin'," The Baby Song from *Oh Brother, Where Art Thou?*, and "Baby, You Can't Love One." But we don't really know all the words to "Baby, You Can't Love One." We make up the one that rhymes with the number four: "Baby you can't love four because you can't fit through the door."

"Why does love make you fat?" Zoe wonders. I think of wine and look at my soft stomach. Why indeed?

"I don't think it's fat so much as you can't fit all four people at once through the door."

"That doesn't make any sense."

"No. It doesn't but neither does five: Can't love five and stay alive."

"Yeah. Love won't kill you."

"No. Probably not," I say. But truly, I don't know. Sometimes, I love my kids so much my heart hurts. Sometimes, I think about how brown the earth, not just Arizona, is becoming and I can't look either Max or Zoe in the eye.

After Sedona, the road turns flat and dismal. Chaparral-dismal— full of the kind of scrub plants and shrubs that hug tightly to the ground, like arctic tundra, but in this case, to stay close to the water and tucked under from the sun, conflating the way a plant grows for why it grows where it does. Like there's no way anyone could grow anything delicious down here, let alone grapes. But then you turn left and find Oak Creek again. Birds fly outwards from the river like there's somewhere better to go. (They figure out quickly that there is not any place better than the river and do an about-face.) To the right, as the road twists by the creek, the riparian vegetation zone abounds with cottonwoods, willows, reeds. To the left, full-on desert sand. You neck is sore, whiplashing as you check the two impossibly paired sights—lush to the right, vapid to the left, abundance to the right, scarcity to the left.

Arizona has a long viticultural history dating from the 16th century when Jesuit priests tended vines and made wine for ceremonial purposes. Most of the grapes in Arizona are grown near Tucson, in the southeastern part of the state. But lately, in the northerly parts between Sedona and Cottonwood, a few pioneer-types grow grapes and make wine. Coming from Oregon, where winegrowing made some sense— 45th parallel and all—I could not imagine what anyone was thinking about trying to grow grapes here. I asked Eric Glomski in what sense it was a good idea to try to grow wine here. Didn't he notice Arizona is, Merriam's six different life-zones notwithstanding, mostly a desert?

He told me actually, grapes don't need that much water, once they're established. I didn't ask how much was not that much. He laughed anyway and said that here in Arizona, his two most difficult weather-related problems were mildew and frost. Unlike in Oregon, when it rains in Arizona, it rains in July and August. This is hard for wine-farmers because late summer is when the grapes need to ripen. It's not so bad for the cabernet grapes. They're loosely packed and can dry out the next morning, but for grapes like pinot noir, it's rough. They're such a tightly compacted grape that when the water gets in, it can't get out. The grapes rot from the inside. And because although this is Arizona, it's still northern Arizona, a frost can creep down the mountain in the night and kill grapes as late as May.

The temperature in Sedona is hotter than in Flagstaff. When it's freezing in Flag, it's usually fifteen degrees warmer. In the summer, when you want it a little hot, it's already too hot in Sedona. A hundred degrees in May. However, Sedona in some ways seems more sustainable—the creek flows through it and plants would have more natural sources of water. I'm a little jealous. Owning a winery, on a spring, next to a creek. Maybe I should move down here.

Born in Chicago, raised in Boston, Glomski went to Prescott, College in Northern Arizona. "Until I moved here, I had no real sense of self and no real sense of place. I majored in landscape ecology. I discovered how important it is to belong somewhere and relate to a landscape. I fell in love with Arizona and shortly after fell in love with wine."

I loved Arizona a little more now that I knew wine could grow here. If Oregon is my Arcadia, my dream of a self-sustaining place, a place where even if the rest of the world fell apart, I could live self-sufficiently, then maybe this little bit of Arizona could be called my Oregon. Here, there are grapes. I could raise honeybees. My dream has always been to have goats. I would milk them. I like goat cheese with my wine.

As Eric and I sat on the deck, my kids ran through the grape vines. Max pinched leaves of sage from the herb garden. He walked over to me, put his fingers in my nose. "Smell my fingers." Eric laughed. It sounded like a pull-my-finger fart joke but Max didn't know that. Zoe looked at Eric, laughing. Did she know the fart joke? No. She didn't She wanted something.

"Can I pick some grapes?" she asked him. She's a little shy. She must have really wanted some grapes to speak to a grown up.

Eric hesitated. "Just a couple. They should be ready." This Arizona winery dream was a good substitute. Eric liked my kids. Maybe I could work here. I clicked through my set of marketable skills—cooking, weeding, braiding hair (good for tending vines?), Photoshopping, wifing (we're both married to other people, but heck, I'm from Utah)—looking for a way to insinuate myself here permanently.

But it was getting hot on the deck. Eric and I, trapped by the niceties of interview, set up our conversation station and that's where we would stay no matter how hot it got or how much wine or water we wanted. Zoe came back over and opened her mouth to ask another question but I shot her a look. I had told both her and Max if they came with me on this interview, they couldn't interrupt. But now that she'd gone back to play, I wondered what she needed.

~

After college, Eric became an ecologist, specializing in river ecology. He spent a lot of time walking up and down rivers. Because pioneers settled along the river, he discovered abandoned homesteads where settlers had left behind orchards of pears, apples and quince that still produced fruit. He started making wine from these fruits. Once he made an apple wine under the tutelage of an apple wine mentor. He remembered tasting the wine and it reminded him exactly of this one homestead he'd found along the creek. The wine tasted just like that place. Those apples tasted only like the apples from that orchard. The wine acted as a conduit of very specific place—you might call it a microclimate. Working as a scientist at the time, the experience was expansive. He came to see the art in the making. "You can paint the landscape, like Monet." Wine gave him the opportunity to be a scientist and an artist and to express the landscape through a liquid. He took time off from teaching at Prescott College and began working at wineries in California. "I really wanted to come back and make wines that expressed *this* place."

"One day I was driving down the road and I saw this place for sale. I had actually hiked along this river before, in my previous life, and looked up here and thought, that is the most beautiful place I had ever seen. I mean, would you ever think we were in Arizona?"

I look around—green vines, green cover crops, maybe alfalfa keeping out weeds from under the vines, shade from the winery and out-buildings, willows hanging over the creek, the creek itself. It's odd to me that to make an Arizonan wine, you have to find some of the least Arizona-like, at least on the surface, land around.

But Eric sees this place as distinctly Arizonan, not because it is sun and desert but because of its nuance. He's found a niche, a fold in the hillside, a bend in the creek where both the possible and the impossible meet. He researched sites all over the state—looking at water supply, soils, geology, elevation, hot and cold temperatures--and then he thought about economic factors, but kept returning to Page Springs. The owners wanted to sell more land than Eric and his partners could afford, but he described his dream, drew a picture of this place for them. He convinced them to sell him just seven acres. The rest he would buy later. "Those owners are kind of like parents to me. They're so proud of what I've done. They come at least once a year to check in and say, 'We're so glad we sold this to you!'"

I'm beginning to see why Eric has been successful. It's optimism mixed with a willingness to give up small parts of the dream if you have to. When you're negotiating a deal, you have to be willing to walk away, and Eric would have built his winery somewhere else if the Page Springs land hadn't worked out. Eric never changed the roots of his dream, but he was willing and able to train the vines up and around his dream.

Now Max and Zoe play hide and seek in the rows of vines. In between, grass. Max trips and falls. And he gets right back up. No rock opening the skin on his forehead this time. Ah, grass in the desert. Maybe dreams can survive climate change. I know that at least rationalization will. We can have grass and wine. We'll just have to learn to like it a little hotter.

"Even with all the research we did, we still got our butts kicked by Mother Nature," Eric told me. You can know everything and still know nothing. Climate is the primary detail with grapes. He chose Page Springs because of the soil, its volcanic material, an extrusive igneous rock, blackish kind of gray basalt. Underneath that basalt is a bed of limestone. Layers of complicated soil make complicated grapes. The Verde Valley used to be an ancient lakebed. The volcanic material flowed on top of it. Limestone is one of the golden jewels of winegrowing. Limestone, because it has a high pH, limits the vigor of the vines. You want the vines to suffer so they will put more energy into the fruit. I know what he's talking about.

Wine grapes are not like food grapes. You want them sweet. You want them seedless. Wine grapes are an extreme, complex fruit. But as a winemaker/artist/scientist, you're choosing a harsh path. The scientist in you is balancing the acids, the sweetness, the yeasts. You measure and you test. The artist in you is looking for an aesthetic. Unlike adapting purely for survival, something else is desired.

The kids are getting hungry and I am getting thirsty. There is wine, El Serrano, and bruschetta, prosciutto and fig with pistachio butter, in the building just a hundred yards up the hill. But this is the dream, sitting on the deck by the creek, watching the kids play, hearing about the acrobatics of wine growing. I sit. I look up the hill. It's not so far. It won't be too long. I'll get to the wine and food soon enough.

Eric pays attention to the bands of elevation too, but not in my anxious, dream-needy way. His obsession isn't mine. His dream isn't a dream of sitting and drinking. It's a dream of making it work. I do get that. I'm married. I'm a writer. I teach. I have kids. We have a house. I'm working all the time. I try to align my obsession with Eric's. Break the mountain into strata, then deal with it. The band of elevation in this state that is conducive to growing grapes is roughly between 3,500 and 5,500 feet. If you go too low, it gets too hot and your grapes lack acidity. Acid is a big part of what makes wine wonderful. Wine is actually quite acidic. The average pH is 3.5—like a mixture of lemon and orange juices. The temperature has to be cold enough to make the grape suffer, to produce acid, to prevent the wine grapes tasting like Welch's. If you go too high, above 5,000 like Munds Park or 7,000 like Flagstaff, you can't actually get the grapes ripe enough. They won't develop enough sugar. The wines would be too acidic. You would also deal with winter kill issues and spring frosts. Down south in Phoenix you also deal with drought and too much heat.

So within this little band of elevation that exists in different spots throughout the state, the wine industry grows. They might have wineries in Phoenix one day, but they're not going to grow great grapes there. Eric works within that band, but there are striations and fluctuations within that band. The winery partners with vineyards in Chiracahua Mountains near Portal that are close to 5,500 feet, but because of the funnel of cold air coming down from Flag, Page Springs suffers more frost here at 4,000 feet.

Eric claims that the distinctiveness of place comes out in the wine. "I've also been most surprised by how unique and distinctive our wines are here. Pinot noir is one of my passions. I can taste pinot from Santa Barbara, from Napa, from Carneros, from the Russian River, and it's pretty easy to tell where those came from. I guess I really look forward to the day when people can say, this came from Arizona." He's looking forward to the day when people can vicariously experience this microclimate in their bottles of wine.

But that variation presents challenging management issue too. If the tiniest variation can lead to different outcomes, then unless you know all the permutations, the outcomes will not turn out as you had hoped. In a little vineyard right below the deck upon which we sit, near the water, there's a gentle slope that leads to the water. Eric planted two varietals, mainly grenache, near the banks of the river where the river materials are mostly gravel and sand. Grenache is known to be incredibly vigorous and the gravel would keep the vines in check, vigor-wise and let the grapes, which like it warm, produce a good mixture of sweetness and acid.

But he was wrong. Lower is not always warmer. The river valley drains cold air all the way from upper Oak Creek and the edge of Flagstaff. Cold air is denser. Each night it literally flows down like water, down this valley bottom. It flows across the bottom of this vineyard planted with grenache, making the bottom of the vineyard radically colder. Eight years later, he still hadn't gotten a crop off those vines.

Eric shakes his head like he can't believe this happened to him, after all that research, after being a river ecologist. I picture the cold coming down like a ghost, nipping those grapes in the bud, forcing their vines to tuck under toward the ground. These grenache were not adapting at all. Even though from where we sit, it's like 102 degrees. If I were a grenache vine, I'd be sprouting grapes out of my sweaty head. But it's the nighttime temperatures that make the grape blossoms stay tucked safely in their vines.

"We tried all these different things—built straw bales to act as a wall, bought a fan that takes air from the ground and shoots it into the sky. Years and years late, we finally said, fuck it. Pulled out those grenache vines one-by-one and planted a French-American hybrid. Gewurztraminer and sauv-blanc. That's just one of many examples that you learn about microclimates by farming. When you live a lifestyle when your economic sustenance is directly link to the cycles of nature, you have no choice but to become very conscious of those things."

It's not the machinations, in the end, that will make a difference. Eric and I can't even manage to move out of the sun in temperatures over a hundred degrees. Humans are too slow to change. What makes me optimistic is this: Eric can imagine the force of cold air, the will of red grapes, the size of a barn, the humidity of a valley, the effect of a slope, the amount of sulfur on a grape, the rate of water flowing through Oak Creek per minute, the burble of the spring, the sway of a cottonwood, the birth of his child, his love of pinot noir, his fascination with old homesteads, the first taste of apple wine. It's the capacity to hold each bit of minutia in the head, the ability to hold every tiny thing together simultaneously. The heat and the mildew, the drought and the rain, the ocotillos and the citrus groves, the bear, the train, the ponderosa. If we begin to notice and to remember every tiny thing, life gets longer, the world gets bigger, we begin to hear the voices of millions of microorganisms in the soil saying, look what I can do. And the humans: Look what I can see. Expand your focus and the world becomes numinous.

But in this very moment, the kids are sweaty. Their faces are flushed in the way only Scandinavian skin flushes—like a sunburn. I have to stop Eric. I know he could explain a lot more about what I want to hear. That wine is a realizable dream—that we won't run out, that I won't have to travel to Syria to see how they make wine in places even hotter than Page Springs, that my kids will have grass and water, that the dream of the future is a lot like my dream of the present. Or he could tell me that this could be the end of wine and the end of rain and the end of children. But I go before he can say either. I leave Eric sitting on the deck and walk toward the fence surrounding the wine property. We walk to the gate that reads, "no alcohol beyond this point" and pass through. I'm wearing sandals, carrying Max, holding Zoe's hand and we trip over rocks and slip on the red desert sand but we go a little faster anyway. There's a long granite rock that reaches out over the water where we can put our toes in.

"It's so cold," Max says as he plunges his feet in. But it's not so cold that he pulls his feet out.

"This is my favorite water," Zoe says. I know. It is the best kind. The river kind that moves around your feet, that cools you down, that isn't so deep you'd drown but isn't so shallow you'll be muddy, where coyote willow grows from the banks and herons hide behind its leaves. Where an eagle flies overhead and the climate is neither hotter nor drier because your toes say it is cold and it is wet. You could stay in this place forever where the dream is that this water is a kind of wine.

◎

Microwind

I inch toward you, girl. I do not go with grace. I have been putting it off, which is not the right thing to do. You are just a baby but even when my baby, whose name means *life* in Greek, hovered in the hospital, I did not want to be hospital bound. I prefer to go. Tubes and trachs and vents are the 21st century chains in this broken world. Still, I should have come right away but I had just been to Tucson where the wind was blowing, where Zoe ate 48 orange Cuties, staving off all scurvy and also whatever diseases everyone else came down with later that week, where my friend from college, Misty, chopped the red bell peppers so tiny all the pesticides disappeared, where the re-routed Colorado sunk into the aquifer and we turned on the hose, brought up that water, made our own canal system in the gravel driveway, and then recycled it ourselves, letting it soak into the ground, back into aquifer from whence it came. I should have gone but I am not sure how much I can help. I do not blow much more than hot air and I don't like to fly. I hate the *I* here. I should have gotten on a plane.

I would go to you girl, girl in California, girl, where the oranges we ate in Tucson came from, where the Colorado goes to, if I knew that my coming would catalyze your alveoli to do their chemical work. If there was something the smell of me could do, the slip of my sweat commingling with the abrasive soap that would make the CO_2 in your lungs convert out of your blood, to pull the oxygen in, if the dust mites on my eyelashes could make nanowork and puff air sacs open better than the ventilator could, if the microorganisms in my gut, keeping me as healthy as any orange Cutie, could bounce into your stomach and train your stomach to pull in the whole round of the world. It's like you've got your soul stuck halfway in and halfway out and you're choking on it, little girl. You've been womb-free for eight weeks, girl, and your eyes are open and looking at your mom whose eyes I won't be able to look into when I tell you, girl, it's not the horror of death you see but the horror of little miracles that are just not getting off the ground. I would like to think that my impending arrival will bump those pneuma from concrete flats into the phenomena they are supposed to be, pneuma from the Greek, the vital spirit; the soul. Or in Theology, the Spirit of God; the Holy Ghost.

I will come anyway and sing a song about being forsaken. In between the lyrics of the song, I will chant words to you. An incantation that I pray will become an incarnation. In that song about flying on the wind I will sing also the word pneuma over and over again. From the Greek: *pneûma,* literally, breath, wind, akin to *pneîn,* to blow, breathe. I will say to you, forget about pneumonia. I will incant to you the pneuma and, in my dreams, it will become your lungs and I will blow myself from here, so far away, to you.

But my song, like everyone who is singing to you, is made of very privileged air. Air goes in. Air goes back out. How reliable. But wind. Wind is what you need. Where does it come from? Where does it go? Wind is its own kind of miracle. Not even the Holy Ghost can blow it himself. Wind is a small miracle and what's going to save you has got to be a little thing. Smaller than you, tiny baby. The smallest thing in the world.

◎

Microgalaxy

It was almost imperceptible the way time slipped from the normal, waiting until her baby is big enough to go home to the waiting until her baby is well enough to go home. It's a different kind of patience, maybe the real patience. The first is: hurry it up, goddamnit. The second is: she comes in at 9:30. She leaves at 5:30. This is her job. My best friend the artist's new job is to sit by the bed of her babies. She may have it for a long time. She might have it forever.

When the girls were born, she could have sworn she heard them both breathe deeply. But a breath taken in does not necessarily carbon dioxide exchange compute. The oxygen didn't last for the first baby. The oxygen the second baby breathed did what it could to redden the blood vessels but the blue veins bringing back the carbon dioxide could not find a way to exhaust. Some newborns get over this quick, this pulmonary hypertension. Not this baby. Her baby's alveoli, sacs of lung, are not making that equal sign in those chemical equations she swore off studying so many high school years ago. By the time of the imperceptible time change, she has studied up on her stoichiometry. She has calculated moles. She has memorized the upper half of the periodic table. She has learned to whisper alveoli as a talisman.

She is glad for her iPhone. She keeps up with the doctors. The doctors didn't know she could spell so well. She didn't know she could type so fast in the middle of the night when the doctors call to say the baby is desatting and does she in fact wish for heroic measures. Wish? No one wishes that one will need a hero. Who is the hero here? Obviously, the galaxy will be the hero—with its nebula and cosmic dust—when the baby pulls through. Obviously, the dark of space will be a gift one day when it stops ringing her awake. It was a strange dream she was having: two girls, her twins, the twins she was going to bring home, playing basketball. One girl blocking the other's pass. The girl still manages to lift the ball into the air and toward the basket but it's not the ball falling through the basket—it's the image of the two suns, one collapsing into the blackhole of the basket, the other going supernova, waves of light burning out the basket, the ball, the blacktop, the mother's own eyes. The baby's eyes are ringing and there's the phone. There's the call she does not want. She would rather return to her dream where babies are metaphors and the only real thing is white sheets warmed by her body's burrowing in. Her chemical signature is inscribed in these sheets. She would like to stay there, with it. She goes to the phone.

She already knows pulmonary. But spell this: Pulmonary lymphangiectasia also known as lymphangiectasis also known as lymphangiomatosis is the diagnosis this night. Here's what the doctors say: rare congenital disease. We'd like to rule it out. She would also like to rule it out. Here is what Google says: PL presents at birth with severe respiratory distress, tachypnea, and cyanosis, with a very high mortality rate at or within a few hours of birth. She Googles tachypnea and cyanosis:

Tachypnea, rapid breathing. Oh, she thinks. Tachy. The nurses use that word all the time to describe her baby's breathing. Tachy up means breathing goes faster, harder, like a bird. A dying, fluttering bird.

Cyanosis. She's a painter. She's seen her baby. She knows that she has been blue. Cyan Cyan Cyan. Cerulean blue.

This is what she doesn't know. How rare? How congenital? This is a rare congenital disease caused, maybe, no one really knows, by the lungs not going through their normal regression period at 20 weeks gestation. What was she doing at 20 weeks, she wonders? She Googles "normal lung regression period at 20 weeks gestation." She gets, during the canalicular phase (16th–26th weeks), differentiation of the epithelial cells lining the alveolar ducts occurs, the first type II cells containing lamellar bodies appear, and capillary growth within the developing lung begins." The capillaries in the lungs are not growing. The alveolar ducts are not venting. The type II cells containing lamellar bodies are what make surfactant. She already knows her baby has a hard time making surfactant.

What she also doesn't know is this: "Although the incidence of these conditions is not directly correlated to the possible incidence of PL, it may be useful to keep in mind that the incidence of hydrops fetalis in obstetric-neonatal referral centers may be as high as 1:800. Furthermore, this condition carries a poor prognosis with a mortality rate ranging from 50% to 98%, and the incidence of congenital chylothorax is about 1:10,000–15,000 pregnancies, with a male-female ratio of 2:1."

She doesn't need to know Latin to know what "hydrops fetalis" means. A water-filled baby. A baby with water where her lungs ought to be. This baby sounds a little too much like her body in the middle of the night. In the middle of the night, when she is sweating and her stomach turns and cramps and threatens to unleash itself upon those white sheets she just one minute ago thought of as comfort are now as diseased as one would-be daughter and the other hard-breathing baby. Maybe the dream meant something. Maybe this word she can now spell reads "twin." She wonders why fetalis and fatalis are so easily exchanged, chemically, in her head.

In the morning, when she has wiped all the fluids away from her own body, when she made it to the hospital to wipe all the fluids off the body of her one daughter, her only daughter, her living twin, another doctor comes in and says, I don't think it's lymphangiectasia.

The doctor jokes, I don't even know how to spell that.

And she says, I do.

But, the doctor says, we've tried three rounds of surfactant replacement therapy. It's not working.

Surfactant decreases surface tension—the word refers to any kind of soapy liquid. Detergents. Surfactants are used to make the cogs turn. Grease the wheels. In humans, the grease is especially cleansing. It makes what would be tacky, sticky, stuck little balloons in the lungs slippery. On a micro-level, the surfactant slides between the stick and tack, and lets the balloons alight letting the alveoli do their clean-up work—bringing the carbon dioxide in to be released, sending oxygen out into the blood vessels. On a larger level, surfactant is necessary to make the lungs compliant—to comply means to expand just the right amount to bring the oxygen in and to let the CO_2 out.

Her baby's lungs do not comply. She thinks, in the dark part of her brain, go ahead, rebel, little rebel. But she doesn't mean it. What she means is, I have better words for it: elastic, flexible, effective. They have given her daughter three doses of replacement surfactant—donated by the kind dead lungs of a pig. There is a disease called surfactant syndrome which means the first type II cells containing lamellar bodies cannot make surfactant. One can't live, or rather, one can't breathe, without surfactant. The lungs flatten like balloons at a birthday party no one is going to.

The doctor says, we gave her one more dose. It's not working anymore. The pig died for nothing. No one is complying, except for maybe the pig. Really, no one is complying at all.

The lymphangiectasia phone call was easier to type than the next phone call: We believe your daughter might have ACD. We will have to do a lung biopsy to confirm. To perform a lung biopsy on a 34-week gestation preemie baby with chronic lung disease who suffers from respiratory distress is a risk. A very, very big risk. But we should find out if she has ACD.

Anyone can spell ACD. Not so many people can stand the definition: Alveolar capillary dysplasia (ACD) which Wikipedia says is a rare, likely congenital, disorder of the lungs and especially of the blood system serving the lungs. It is a disorder of the newborn. The normal diffusion process of oxygen from the air sacs to the blood in the lungs and, thence, to the heart, fails to develop properly. The disorder is sometimes called misalignment of the pulmonary veins. Rather than misaligned, the pulmonary vein is malpositioned in a site somewhat different from its normal position.

Infants with the disorder present with the signs of lack of oxygen (hypoxemia) and severely increased pulmonary hypertension. Since treatment is seldom, if ever, effective, life expectancy of the infant is very, very, short.

Wikipedia says the longest living survivor of ACD was two months old. Can she imagine, waiting in the hospital with the diagnosis of probable ACD hanging over her head, over the head of her baby, with the threat of an unnecessary lung biopsy lurking with the question of why bother, we'll know in two months whether it is ACD or not ACD?

I suspect that she can imagine. I suspect she knows. I suspect that the wait to find out would very, very hard. Almost as hard as doing no lung biopsy at all and just waiting to see. She's already almost two months old. If she makes it past two months old, does that reverse the diagnosis? We would like some rules. Some clear, strict rules, like the rules for stoichiometry.

It is so rare, so rare, these diseases so rare. But she is getting better. They want to take the baby off the jet ventilator. But just before they do, they want to run one more test—one more baby CT scan to see if her baby has something called Interstitial Fibrosis in Newborns. She can type that one—that one she is sure has a cure. She knows to always type "in newborns." Diseases of the newborns do not present like diseases of the awhile-ago born. She knows the symptoms: tachynea, cyanosis, respiratory distress syndrome. Word for word in every diagnosis. This one has treatment: inhaled steroids. Steroids make her nervous. The baby already has an infection. The doctors are already giving her antibiotics. She knows to give an infection a steroid is like giving the infection a big bowl of Wheaties. She knows infection can lead to pneumonia. She knows pneumonia can lead to atelectasis. She knows lungs collapse and the alveoli sacs can fall down into themselves and not lift back up. She knows the baby is tired from all this work and that she could use a big bowl of something herself, her own Wheaties, preferably not a steroid, to give her the energy to inflate those lungs, transfer oxygen to the blood vessels, remove carbon dioxide from the veins. Every single gas exchange is something the baby has to consider and her mom can't do her thinking for her. All she can do is wait to see if this new diagnosis can be ruled in or ruled out. Interstitial is a word she likes better than the others but is still not the word she wants to hear which is *breathe* and *home*. She decides to wait and see. No steroid. If the baby gets better, then, once again, what she has or had is not that.

Dr. Lou is angry at the artist-painter for not agreeing to the CT scan. Dr. Lou doesn't care about the radiation. Dr. Lou doesn't care when she voiced concern about the steroid dexamethasone, which has been suspected to cause severe neurological effects in children. Dr. Lou doesn't care because she still doesn't believe this baby is going home. She told her so, to her face. She said, she is still a very sick baby and when Dr. Lou said *baby* she could not hear in Dr. Lou's voice that flip of a stomach that we all hear when we hear baby and think baby, I love babies, and the fact that the baby is still in the hospital is to her a given not a not given, not a not fair, not a not real. Dr. Lou says the word atelectasis. Dr. Lou doesn't say collapsed lung because she doesn't know what it's like to collapse. I know the word atelectasis. My baby was collapsing alveoli all over the place. I brought my baby to her this week so she could see her now, at six years old, what she is waiting to have in the future, but now I see that she may also see in my girl all that she may not have, even for all this waiting, even for this new patience, this kind of patience that wakes up in the morning, thinks, breathe, steps into the shower, breathe, shampoo in hands, breathe, suds in hair breathe, no conditioner, no one cares, breathe, brush teeth, breathe, breathe on Dr. Lou, breathe, eat a bite of banana, breathe, eat another bite of banana breathe, quit eating banana because it's too tiring, breathe, look for car keys, breathe, look for iPhone because there is no other waiting friend better than the phone that will take her to Google so she can spell her newfound, hateful words, breathe, drive left, breathe, girl, breathe, drive right, breathe girl, that car in front of her had better not stop because she's breathing on behalf of a baby who is in the NICU in California and traffic is not part of the patience, not part of the diagnosis. The only diagnosis today is sign in to the hospital, wash her hands for two-and-a-half minutes, up to the elbows, sign in again, talk to the nurse, sing to her baby, Google words she wishes she never had learned to spell, be afraid all the time, wish she had a ventilator for herself, be afraid and hopeful that one day all this waiting will change imperceptibly to that kind of waiting where it's not waiting to heal, just waiting to grow.

One day, they will tell her, go get the car seat. She'll be as surprised as she was the day they said, let's take her off the vent. She'll be as surprised as the night she got the phone call saying, we were wrong, it's not ACD. She'll be as surprised as she was the evening her babies were born and she heard them inhale and the exhale tumbled right after it. As surprised as she was that she could make at least one daughter reach two-months old. As surprised as she was, two days after they extubated that baby to see her breathe as if she hadn't been waiting to catch her breath at all.

◎

Microwindmills

A few miles past Cameron and the bridge that takes you over the almost-always-empty Little Colorado, there's a house that's been under construction for as long as I've driven route 89 between here and the vermillion cliffs. The face of the house is full of features, like the cliffs toward which I drive. It's hard not to notice two-story tall Navajos, painted flat, their photographic faces pressed into plywood. The man wears a cowboy hat, the woman, a bandana. I only think they're Navajo because the house is being constructed on the reservation and their skin is as weathered as that plywood. Cynthia Yazzie, a student of mine, works at Kohl's and writes lines of poems that do so much undoing and see so much unseeing that they suck the air out of the room. She hates the painted bodies on the forever-under-construction house. Because they lie, she says. There are no two-storied Navajos out on the reservation. No one would pose that tall. No one would paint that weather. There aren't even any two-storied houses constructed on the reservation. On the top of the mostly mobile, one-story houses, empty tires line roofs. On mobile homes, the sheet metal roof skin is screwed in only on the perimeter, not across the top of the trusses. The tires prevent roof rumbling in the high winds. Sheet metal makes its own business, reminding the house dwellers exactly where they live which is helpful because out here, in this hundred and twenty miles of crumbling red cliffs, there are no trees to let you see the wind.

◎

Microhematocrit

It is possible that there is not one word that cannot host a micro in front of it. The only things I can think of are real nouns-things you can eat. I cannot eat a hematocrit but I can micro it. Micro is the domain of the elusive, the abstract, the plausible but not the palpable. When does the micro ever really matter? Perhaps only when its meaning is displaced. Microbrew. It's not that the beer is tiny. The micro is not Budweiser. Not Coors. Sometimes micro is merely a correction. I do not eat microberries, micropotatoes, microtoast, microsteak.

On a Tuesday in the fall, any fall, it doesn't matter, fall is always dying, dying is worse than dead, and therefore, as beautiful as fall is, winter is still not as terrifying, I thought I was dying. There was a lump, there was a test, an X-ray, an electrocardiogram. There was the move, the leaving, the new air, the lack of red only yellow aspens, brown gambel oaks, there was only railroad and freeway. There was only doctor after doctor and then, only then, smaller copays and larger appointments, the kind that filled hours and required out-patient. How could I die so many ways in just one year? I held my cat close to me because he, I knew, would die before me and I could gauge my fear in the thinness of his skin, the rosary of his bones. His teeth were covered in tiny dots of red. It was not the red I had been missing. I missed his large orange fur. The markings that made him look like an ocelot. I missed the things I could see.

◎

Microsoccer

I tried to bring a book. I tried to bring a chair. I tried to talk to the other moms. I tried to talk to the dads. I tried to bring the team snack but failed, bringing carrots. I tried to get a sense that you can't kick the ball first if you're the one who kicked it off but I think I have that wrong too. I tried to pull the grass and eat the milky ends but there was elk shit all over and dog piss probably too. Really, there was nothing to eat except carrots, and therefore, I had a hard time paying attention. She didn't kick the ball hard enough and when she did kick it, the ball went out of bounds. Sometimes, she kicked it the wrong direction. Sometimes, someone kicked it hard in the wrong direction and all the kids ran all the way out of bounds, offsides, down the hill, over elk shit and dog piss chasing a ball that would never come back. For me, it was good for a metaphor anyway—chasing youth or boys or of hungry members of the Cervidae family looking for edible grass on the other side of the mountain where perhaps the fire or the drought didn't wipe all the grass out.

I apologize. I need to apply some kind of drama because I wasn't going to get up off my chair or put down my book and join them in chasing that ball. I knew I'd never catch it and the team would never forgive me for getting in the way of a game whose rules have nothing to do with how to feed so many animals with so many feet.

◎

Microtrain

A regular-sized train can't do it. The tracks crisscross in too many layers. There is not enough money in the world to build four million bridges deep. But if the train is small enough, fiber optic, microscopic, the tracks could bend and weave and thread. Instead of stopping at crossings for cars or for anti-abortion protesters, the veins could thread like those in a body. In that body, red could stand for oxygen and blue for carbon dioxide and the world would be happy to get and return either. In a body, the reliance on input and output would be a fair and reasonable thing. In the lungs, the carbon dioxide exchanges for oxygen with the justice of stoichiometry. Transformation is always possible. The oxygen has persuasive arguments. The CO_2 has its own. No cell changes its body, it just changes its mind. This body holds its power in its tiny mitochondrial engines—forward moving but not at anyone else's great expense. This is a kind of country I could live in. One day, it will be small enough.

◎

Microblogs

Because *Scientific American* reports a study that found that people recall Facebook status updates more readily than they recall information read from a book. Because *Scientific American* calls Facebook posts Microblogs. Because microblogs resemble ordinary speech. Because microblogs say what you mean and don't try to be fancy. Because there is already someone to listen. Because the word "sepulcher" is never used. Because books are sepulchers. Because the word "shimmering," a word often used in books of poetry, is rarely used in status updates and if it is so used it is easy to unfriend the user. Because the politics are already agreed upon. Because the cadence is the cadence of early humans. Because the early humans communicated contextually. Because the context is a face. Because a face is easy to remember. Because a friend is someone who says things you like. Although the scientists didn't think humans would remember words written in such haste. Because the scientists are often surprised. Because what is more important than something written in haste, but that it is hastily read? Because teachers might incorporate this into their lessons. Because students are early humans too. Because I will teach a class on this. Because my students would like the class to read a microblog full of context and care and faces. Because the world needs more faces. Because the world needs more, if shorter, words. Because I can remember what you said in your last Facebook post about those with the smallest hearts have the greatest freedom I can't remember who posted it and although I can't remember what famous writer said it first but I can remember each of the words in the exact right order which is more than I can say about anything I wrote except maybe the one day I wrote a Facebook post about being so tired I wanted to put my head in a bucket of sleep and the words were well-liked and I was well-liked and I went into the day tired but finally, for what seemed like the first time, read. And, according to *Scientific American*, my Facebook friends will indeed remember about sleep and buckets but you, reader, will not remember this essay because it is longer than the accepted word length of a microblog and it is full of long sentences and words I don't even remember. Because neither you nor I will remember who wrote the article in the *Scientific American* or who did the research or who invented Facebook but I will remember to friend you when I get home so I can begin to remember you.

◎

Microfire

It started small. Not two kids with rubbing sticks. Not two members from the Navajo Nation setting pranks behind dumpsters. Not two ATV riders with very sunburnt necks sparking their batteries. Not two hippies who spaced putting sand on their fire. Not even overachieving squirrels. Not ravens with a match. No, there was no direct cause for this fire that is burning over 7,000 acres, for this fire that is the Bambi Disney version, forcing squirrels and skunks and raccoons to flee and *is also not* Disney-like in that humans evacuate their fire-magnetic homes and shelter at the Yavapai Community Center. Take refuge. Get away.

Evacuations are not all that rare anymore. Last year, the big fire out by Payson, and two years ago, the Wallow fire, largest fire in Arizona history, and three years ago the Schultz fire and then also the one that had our housesitter packing up her car with all the pictures she could find of our kids and the pictures that our kids had drawn and the things that looked like important pieces of paper, drawn by the kids or not, as she frantically tried to call us as we camped so ignorantly out by Sycamore Point just thirteen miles away but too far for cell service and too far to know that the fire called Little America was turning towards us and the winds were up and the humidity low and in June in Arizona you should know better and keep a pack of memorabilia packed and ready to go because you are human and you will forget everything that you ever learned without a piece of paper on which to write it down.

You had better treasure that paper. The trees. They are burning down. The trees, some say, will not come back. The trees need certain conditions. Some humidity. Some rain. Some days where temperatures are below 32 degrees. Other plants may grow. Juniper and chaparral. Pinyon Pine. Maybe we can make paper out of juniper upon which we can invest our memories and protect them from a fire that is coming since fires like that just aren't that rare anymore.

In Prescott, no one is blaming anyone directly. At the Yavapai Community Center, a man sits on the edge of his cot. Another man stands a couple of miles away, white lines through black ash. In the Center, a woman quiets her baby. The baby is hot and the corner seems the coolest, quietest space. Back at the fire, a woman digs her Hotshot shovel into the ground. Fire lines. They used to work. Maybe they will work today. There is another man, a fire detective, walking the line between forest and the Center. In between, he will find the cause, but never a direct one. Human-caused for sure. All the fires now. Just touch the air. Touch the ground. It hasn't rained for months. The humans are good at so many things: starting fires and stopping rain.

◎

Microtopography

When I was thirteen, my boyfriend's mother used to drive us to Sugarhouse Park. At Sugarhouse Park, she would sit us next to the rocks by the river. The river came from the mountains. The river came over the rocks. The rocks made the river flow hard. The rocks gave the river what gravity and slope couldn't. Bubbles. My boyfriend's mother made us sit by the bubbles to inhale the negative ions that she promised would make us happy. We sat by the river as it rushed and as it bubbled. We breathed in the bubbles, happily. On the ride home, my boyfriend drove. I sat in the middle. His mother sat to my right. I held a bag of Doritos between my legs. He fished for chips. He fished with his finger. His eyes looked straight ahead but his finger never stopped. His mother told us about a river too far away where the water fell fifty feet. The whole canyon was full of ions, negative ones, looking for some positive ion to catch itself onto, to tickle its magnet, to pull the whole fabric closer to its edge, to threaten to punch through the plastic and make something purely invented, real.

Micromeasures

Cari is an administrator. She is very organized, very thin, and very beautiful. She is also very quiet and reserved. Or so I thought, but when I met with her in her office to ask how to best go about changing our MA to an MFA she said, easy. Name change. And then she sat me down to ask how I had been since last we worked on that committee together. I said, *fine how are you,* and she said, *good,* she loved her job as administrator and she loved her husband who was a lawyer. Their kids were just a bit older than my kids, maybe that's why we sat down, to talk about kids, but I brought up how my grandma had just died and then she brought up how her best friend had just died. Her friend had developed a virulent breast cancer but the friend could not say aloud that she was dying. She too, like us, had kids and a husband and she too loved her job and she did not want to die so when the doctors in America said there's nothing we can do for you, the doctors practicing a differently organized, alternative medicine in Mexico said, no no, we will save you. They laid her down and put a glass upon her breast. Under the glass swarmed a dozen bees. The bees stung and stung, trying to sting the cancer out of her. The body, stung by the bees, retreated into submission. But the cancer, more organized than the bees, did not. The cancer killed her like the cancer does. She died in Mexico without her husband or her children, with her breast, swollen, expanded and stoic, an erect testament to the attempt to keep things together.

Cari went down to collect her friends' body. Cari, thin as glass, put her head against her friend's chest. She knew she was dead but she swore she heard inside the ribs a swarming sound. She couldn't lift her friend's swollen body but she could take home, in a jar, a handful of bees, their hind ends wet with blood and cancer. Stinger-less, the bees lived while Cari drove to the airport, crossed the border, shuttled up the mountain, and returned to her office where she sat the jar on her desk, and, before her next meeting, held the glass to her face until the bees made enough noise to make a sound like Cari's friend's name.

◎

Microgas

Fry's has the cheapest gas in town—cheaper still if you have fuel rewards from doing all your grocery shopping at Fry's. The grocery store is one of the best places to get all self-righteous. Look at my cart, it's full of blueberries, raspberries, peaches, tomatoes, organic broccoli, free-range chicken, orange juice not-from-concentrate, recycled napkins. You with your Stouffer's and Lean Cuisine and Keebler products. How will you manage all that recycling? How will you metabolize all that sugar and salt? Look at my grocery bags—canvas and brought from home. Oh, I see you didn't bring yours. You know, don't you, that Fry's wraps one item per plastic bag? I see you don't know that it takes a thousand years for each of those bags to decompose. I see that you don't know that precious gasoline goes into making those bags every second. Oh. You see that I'm filling up my car with some of that precious gasoline. But at least I don't drive a Suburban like you or leave it running in the parking lot while you take your child into day care. I have a dream to climb into the driver's seat and turn your car around or move it three spaces down. Small subversions. But yes, you're right, I'm still filling up my car with gas. I am driving to the same places you're driving. I'm ferrying groceries.

I'm taking my kids to school and dance. I'm yelling at the car in front of me to please for Chrissakes do you not know what a signal is?

And then I see you, out of the corner of my eye, take the empty plastic water bottles out of the hands of the woman who was walking them toward the trash can. I hear you say, "It's fine. I have a big recycling bin. I'm happy to take them for you. It's hard to recycle when you're on the road." And then I see this human. The one small thing. Her heart as big as a recycling bin. I finish filling up my car. I drive back over, a whole twenty feet or so. I let the car idle. I go back in the store, not a single canvas bag in hand. I head to the frozen food aisle. Stouffer's and Stouffer's and Stouffer's for all.

◎

Microisland

Margie and I talked about the weather. It was raining at five in the afternoon. "My friend Fredricka, who lives next store and who has been here thirty years, said during monsoon, it would rain like clockwork from one until three and then you could go about your business. Now, you can't tell when a storm is coming."

"It's happening everywhere. In Iowa, summer is so long now," Margie says. Margie is from Manila. She says her friends in the Philippines don't care about climate change. "These are people on an island! They're going to get sunk first." We laughed. Possibly nervously. She told me about a tiny island she visits every couple of years. A four-hundred-year old Balete tree sits in the middle of the island. When Margie was young, her family would come for picnics and to swim and to sit under the long arms of the Balete. Now, the water is up to the roots of the tree. Soon, the salt water will erode the roots and the tree will fall down. "I take people there to see it. I say, look, there goes our tree." But they don't see it. Not even as it sinks right before their eyes. Maybe they think their own islands will be lifted up in some kind of scales of justice kind of balance. Maybe all our feet are getting wet and we stand around and blame the sand for not being a little bit sturdier.

Microspikes

Janice Romick is a saver of the bees. She plants lavender, mint, and sunflowers around the hexagonal patio of her condominium. She would plant artichokes, if they could grow well around a patio in Utah, so she could see the bees tumble upside-down in the overgrown thistle. She loves to imagine the comfort the needly purple petals provide to needled bee bodies. She's stopped using Roundup on the dandelions that grow in the patio's cracks. Stopped making calls on her cell phone. She has done everything she can think to stop disrupting the bee colonies but she knows she is just one and there are too many disruptions to try to think about the bees every day, anyway.

Inside her house, a yellow jacket bounces against the window shaped like a hexagon that looks from the inside out to the yard. The yellow jacket slides up the glass and down until she's certain it can't make its way out on its own. She picks up a paper napkin—the cheap, not even recycled kind—and approaches the yellow jacket fast and confident, pinching it with her fingers. Not too hard. Gently. She lifts the napkin, opens the door that leads to the patio. and lets the yellow jacket free into the relative safety of the mint.

She does this a lot. She's been stung a few times. She's not sure why the yellow jackets persist in coming into her house. Perhaps they plan to colonize her home, her house a hexagon, her house of windows, her house of doors that does good work to keep the disruptions out.

She thinks she can probably get along with them just fine as long as she doesn't bother them or they her. But that's the hard thing. Figuring out which of you is the poked and which the poker. What is the inside of the giant honeycomb and what is the out.

◎

Distracted Parents of the Micromanagement Era

Rebecca

"My gallery is showing the cool kids now. I am definitely not one of the cool kids. They think I'm a mom."

"You are a mom. Do they have a cool moms show?"

"They definitely do not have a cool moms show."

"You just painted Madonna wrapped in Christmas lights. What kind of mom would paint that?"

"What kind indeed?"

This was later, after her third child died thirty-six hours after her birth and her fourth child had been rushed from the Santa Monica hospital to the Children's Hospital Los Angeles. After that child lived and after that child came home and after that child survived a whole winter season without contracting RSV—the respiratory infection that would have sent her back to Children's. Back to the vent.

Before the after: Rebecca sat on the edge of the full-size bed her six-pound daughter lay upon. The daughter needed the whole bed, not for her size, but for her ventilator. Called a high frequency ventilator, or a jet ventilator, this mechanical ventilator uses a respiratory rate greater than four times the normal breathing, about 150 breaths per minute at very small tidal volumes. High frequency ventilation reduces lung injuries like hypoxemia and widespread capillary leakage. The sound is similar to a small jet engine preparing for takeoff. I have been here for one hour and already I have had no thoughts except, "get me out of here, get me out of here." Rebecca has been here for four months. I wonder if the sound of the jet has pummeled all the thoughts out of her.

Rebecca is a better mother than I am. When my daughter Zoe was in the hospital, I snuck in wine. I snuck in work. I graded papers and wrote book reviews. I am not a singular thinker. Rebecca is. She sells a single painting for more than I make in one year but here she is, not painting. Not working. She is not knitting. Not watching TV. Not reading a book. She looks at her daughter, Andi. "Her skin looks kind of pale, doesn't it?"

Her skin actually looks kind of red, the same color red as when Zoe was in the NICU, having been born too early, like Andi, and her skin not ready for the dry world. Her skin, like Andi's, should have remained in the wet world. But I don't know what Andi looked like yesterday. I just got here. Rebecca leaves me alone with the jet and the baby, who has a kind of pulmonary edema and maybe a hundred other problems, so she can talk to the doctor. I force myself to stare at her skin to see if it changes color, but I'm already looking at the monitors, at the TV, at my phone. I will do anything to get out of here, even if my body stays.

Rebecca comes back with the doctor who, like me, cannot judge Andi's pallor. Rebecca is the painter. She knows color. The doctor looks away from Andi and looks at Rebecca, listing a whole new array of possible diseases Andi may have. Like me, the doctor doesn't want to focus. She wants to duck into the escape of her brain and demonstrate how diagnostic, how associative, how fully connected all these dots of information may be.

"I think we should turn down the vent," Rebecca suggests. She's not the doctor but she's the only one paying attention.

Later, a different doctor comes in. "We turned down Andi's vent."

"Good, thanks." Rebecca nodded.

"And then we noticed her sats stayed up." *Sats* mean oxygen saturation, I knew from Zoe's NICU stay.

"That is also good."

"We think we're going to take her off the vent tonight."

I jump up to give Rebecca a hug. Finally. After four months. She's going to be free. But Rebecca has a different patience. She looks at Andi's skin. "We'll see how her color stays." Rebecca can paint an entire eight by twelve-foot canvas one day and, upon returning to the studio the next, "wipe the whole thing clean and start over." She is a doctor of pallor and patience. She can decide when to take Andi off the vent.

Sarah

In the visitor room, sitting across from him, only the first time since he'd been sentenced, Sarah put a notebook between her and her dad. He was in minimum security. No bars. No glass walls. So paper was all she could use to protect herself. She asked him the questions in the most journalistic type manner.

"Did you say you'd hurt her if she told?"

"Sarah, I am so sorry."

"Is it youth? Or is it power?"

"Sarah. Please forgive me."

"Do you feel you perpetrated your offenses because offenses were perpetrated against you?"

"Sarah. I am sorry."

"Did you ever think about me, Dad?"

Neither of them knows if she means as one of his victims or as his daughter who now lives without her dad.

Sarah researched counselors who work with sex offenders. She once told me that the counselors themselves have a hard time telling others what they do. Almost as outcast, their puerile jokes are understood as letting off steam. Bananas and too-small holes in donuts. Sarah picks her notebook up and writes the joke

Michelle

She isn't usually called to crises anymore. As Arizona Domestic Violence Fatality Assessor, she arrives after the fact. She meets with the DA and the local police, the FBI, social services, domestic violence shelters, and victim witness programs to figure out what went wrong, where social services might have intervened earlier. But this day, her previous boss Myra was out on a call and Mark the FBI guy had her number on speed dial and called her. There had been a shooting. Kids were at the home. Could she come talk to them?

Michelle has her own kids. They are my kids' ages. Both boys, they have longish wavy hair. Zoe and Liam play walkie-talkies. They build houses of mud for roly polies even though Michelle and I object to that name. "They are potato bugs," we argue. They shake their heads. "Roly poly." Our power as parents is incredibly limited. All four children like pizza. Liam and Ian only like cheese pizza. Max and Zoe only like pepperoni. Ordering two pizzas is influence as we have. When I tell them to quit jumping on the bed, they jump more quietly. I despair. Michelle tells them to jump outside. They find puddles. We shake our heads and hide out on the deck.

How much influence? She arrives at the scene. Two kids in regular Superman and Spiderman T-shirts sit on a regular picnic table and eat

174

regular M&M's that the police officer who watched them gave them while they waited for Michelle who will stall until Social Services shows up.

"Hey, I'm Michelle," she tells the kids. She gives them a wave. "You guys doing OK?" Michelle has the most soothing hello. She tilts her head. She smiles until her dimples crack. Everyone she meets wants to move into those dimples and stay there. They are happy and sweet. Better than M&M's. The kids slide over to make room for her.

"I'm sorry about your mom," she tells them.

She doesn't gloss over anything. Their mom has just been taken away by ambulance. Their dad has just been taken away by police. "I want you guys to put this image in your head. Do you remember when your mom took you to the park?"

The kids nod.

"Picture her making your dinner. What's your favorite dinner?"

"Macaroni and cheese."

"Does she add extra cheese?"

Both kids nod.

"I do that with my kids too. Lots of extra cheddar."

The mom may not make it, Mac had told her. Michelle thinks about the Spiderman gloves her son Ian gave her as she left him at preschool. "These will catch your dreams," he tells her. Her only dream is this mom lives. She would like to please not assess a fatality, not this day. When the county social worker shows up, Michelle gets up from the picnic table, tells the boys to remember to picture their mom talking on the phone, tucking her hair behind her ear, drawing around their hands to make turkeys at Thanksgiving. She tells the social worker they like mac and cheese. She thinks hard about her son. His Spiderman gloves. How red they are. Great lines of black interweaving stripes. Even a little rubber on the palm-side for traction. These are great gloves. Very great gloves, she thinks. She puts them on, turns on her car, and drives toward home.

Manuel

Manuel follows the farm manager out to see the cherries. He has been gone from the farm since March. He had heard about the destruction. From the airplane, he had seen the damage. Where there were once only canopies of coffee leaves, now he could see the ground. Half the plants that still had leaves were yellowed. His green green Ahuachapan now an autumnal New England. During the Civil War it had been bad. The army had torched some coffee farms to rout out the guerrillas. But then, so had the FMLN. For them, coffee was the problem. The rich 2% owned the plantations. The other 98% worked them. Or worse, didn't. Extreme poverty drives people to extreme farming. Anti-farming. Burning down the house you live in doesn't seem like a bad idea if your house is made out of cardboard. Most of this was before Manuel's time. He inherited the coffee farm from his parents. A few acres here, another few acres there.

The coffee he grows in the lowlands, he sells to local coffee mills—big enterprises Some of the plants are resistant. He takes a seedling from one of the resistant plants to the greenhouse, packs the dirt around it with two praying hands.

The rust *Hemileia vastatrix* is a fungus that likes water but isn't water dependent. It likes the tropics. It likes Central America. It likes South America. The only America it doesn't like is maybe North, but it even has a little bit of love for Mexico. Manuel lives in Flagstaff, Arizona. It's hard to keep check on a fungus that lives on the other side of the equator—especially a fungus that loves warm temperatures.

The fungus has always existed. Kept in check by some coffee plants' natural resistances and by climate, the fungus was chronic but not lethal. But as the temperatures click up, the fungus has begun to decimate plantations. In the past five years, temperatures have risen from an average of twenty to twenty-five degrees Celsius in the summer to twenty-six to twenty-eight. Two degrees Celsius turns a chronic fungus into a deadly one. What was once nearly impenetrable wall-to-wall green is now a walkable park. Or perhaps, more appropriately, a cemetery. Fungus-ridden plants droop like decaying flowers left behind on Memorial Day—no grave-tender to bury them. Thick vines and branches tip like uneven headstones. It doesn't make you want a cup of coffee. It makes you want a big glass of wine. Maybe whole bottles of it. Perhaps this is the beginning of the end. Perhaps this is the end of the end. Perhaps this is the problem. We want to wait and see how bad things will get. Rubberneckers, we are. It's so exciting, this world-ending. Except it's hard to get excited when there's no coffee to drink.

Sarah

Paper. She was eight when he was convicted and sent tell anyone where her father was or why he was there. Her mother at working twelve-hour days at the bank, she walked the seven blocks from school to the library every day. The only person walking in downtown Phoenix. The only person with secrets so big she had to tuck it under her armpit, stuff it into her backpack, and slip it into her pocket. It went everywhere she did. Even into the library.

That's where it started. The secret spilling out. She drenched the library with it. All that paper sopping up a secreting secret. Her dad should not have put his finger there. So, instead, she put kept her mouth shut but her pen open. Her dad wouldn't confess so she became a writer and confessed for him. On the back of that paper, she flooded his secret. Her dad had his own underworld. In another letter from a man who she once called her father now she calls Bill because now he was paper and she could fold him in her wallet and keep him tucked away. It was clean paper she wanted. The librarian gave her sheaf after sheaf but what she really wanted was sheath. She was the knife. The library, her sheath.

Dangerous with secret. Bubbling over with possibility. She loved the librarian as much as she loved her father who she once knew and now foreigned. She wrote to him like you would write to an ambassador from China. Dear China, please don't drive cars. We need to stop this global warming. Dear Dad, please keep your fingers out of little girls. Dear Brazil, we really need your forests, please don't chop them down. Dear Dad, please come home and be a different person. Dear India, could you please clamp down on that ocean polluting? Dear Dad, could I please have a dad named Bill?

We all write letters on the off chance that the impossible can be made real. Type it in a library. Make the paper bear our burdens and change the world. Or at least the names.

Manuel

Manuel's daughter Ella has just returned from El Salvador. She is as beautiful an eighteen-year-old as I have ever seen, plus, she is shorter than me so I am bound to like her. As I'm talking with Manuel about the great glut of 1996 when Vietnam started exporting coffee beans and coffee that had been selling for twelve dollars a pound sold for $2.54 a pound. Ella's busy uploading pictures of her trip but when I ask Manuel how long he's away from Flagstaff and in Costa Rica, she says, "Five months. From November to March. Every year."

"Do you come back for Christmas?" I ask.

Manuel shakes his head *no*.

"Do you guys go down?" I ask Ella.

"No, it's too expensive. We have school."

I wonder which is more prescriptive—the Flagstaff Unified School District or this farm under attack from this fungus. Manuel has to go back to Ahuachapan. His farm has survived the Civil War. It has survived Vietnam. It has survived privatization and threats of communalization. But this fungus. It takes a whole father away from his whole family for almost half the year. No one seems too sad about it. That's life. They adjust. I can't imagine being away from Erik and my kids that long but I have an addictive personality. I don't dream of a fungus corroding all my parents ever worked for. I stay home, fungus free.

Michelle

Michelle drives to Phoenix once a week. She stopped smoking a long time ago, but now she is in the car so long, the window so crackable, the radio so singalongable, full of the fleeting feeling that she doesn't have a care in the world, including dying, she can't help but smoke.

Michelle never tells anyone what she does—it invites too many questions, involves too many secrets unveiled. She asks my friends when she's over for a barbecue, oh what do you do, what do you do? She deflects with generalities—I'm a social worker so she doesn't have to explain she has a job with the words "fatality" or "domestic violence" in its title.

When she gets to Sierra Vista, just south of Phoenix, she meets with Mark the FBI agent and the DA and the woman from Children and Family Services. They open the file to a pile of pictures of a woman bruised from head to toe.

"It looks like she's been in a car accident," the new assistant district attorney says.

It always looks like that, Michelle thinks.

Michelle looks at the woman's hands. Defensive wounds. Nicotine stains. Wedding ring. Her hands look like her own hands. They look like everybody's hands. Over the glossy photo paper, she pets them a little, as if fingers on photo paper can be soothed.

When she gets home, later that night, she airs out the car as well as she can but her kids know she smokes. All kids can tell.

Sarah

Even the bad dads die. Sarah hadn't seen him in years. Her mother divorced him when he was in prison. His daughters, even the ones he didn't touch, didn't see him after he got out. He would call. But a busy signal is a thing of the past. Call waiting. You don't even have to pick up the phone. Nonstop ringing. Everybody's home.

Her father's girlfriend, or maybe just the girl he was living with, stabbed him. She wanted his money or his drugs or his kindness. You can't get anything just by asking for it these days. Although stabbing and jabbing and tickling with your fingers don't get you very far. The girlfriend lost the money. The father lost his daughters. The daughters called the mother when the coroner called them. The mother, like my mother, divorced but really never, arranged the funeral and paid off the father's outstanding bills because no one should decompose in debt.

Sarah wrote a book of poems and in doing so, forgave his other debt. She claims her father in fire, in plant, in skin, in tree, in warming, and in globe. It's easy to love a father now that he is gone and you don't expect anything— no check, no letter, no poem— in the mail.

Rebecca

Rebecca is canning six-hundred-and-seventy-two pounds of peaches for an art show. Five friends will arrive on July 29th to help her boil Mason jars, sanitize lids, slice peaches, dissolve sugar. I am not one of those friends and I feel guilty from five-hundred miles away. If you are too busy micromanagining your own life to help your friend put up six-hundred-and-seventy-two pounds of peaches in the name of art, what kind of friend are you?

Rebecca posted pictures of the crates of peaches. Ten cardboard crates of peaches sit on tarps to protect the floors from smashed peaches. Andi, her daughter, her third child, the one who survived, pats the top of the crates like she is destined to eat every one. You can be a mama and an artist, as long as you have faith. Which is the point. Raised Mormon,

Rebecca's art comes from the crucible of be-a-good-girl and you-can-do-whatever-you-set-your-mind-to. Set your mind against this hard thought. It will leak like a peach. Mormons are a stubborn lot—they believe they will persist beyond the rest of us in the rapture. One of the comments on the photos on Facebook read, "Your Mormon is showing." Enough peaches to get her to her next show. Enough peaches to feed the daughter who almost did not survive far into the future. Enough peaches to persist through the rapture. Rebecca has covered all her bases and I want to call her so but no one wants to hold a phone with sticky fingers so I watch for updates on Facebook and feel so bad I'm not there. If you cannot help your friend preserve six-hundred-and-seventy-two pounds of peaches in the name of the End Times what kind of friend are you? You forward her pictures of the one peach ripening on your kitchen counter. Scarcity and abundance. Between the two of you, you'll figure out some kind of balance.

◎

Microhaboobs

My next-door neighbors, invited their friends, Baaqir and his wife, to come up to Flagstaff from Phoenix to escape the heat while they attended a wedding in Turkey. I met Baaqir when he asked me what day he should pull out the recycling bins. "Tuesday," I told him.

"I'm glad I didn't miss it," he said.

"You guys liking this weather?" It was 78 degrees in Flagstaff that day. 108 in Phoenix.

"Oh, we love Flagstaff. And it's so good to get away from the haboobs."

I asked him if he'd been in one. He said eight now, all in the last two years. He had lived in Phoenix for ten years. When the most recent haboob came, Baaqir finally felt at home. The size of it. He could see the dust swarming from his house in Scottsdale as it started trucking in from the west. The black tidal energy looked like the worst nightmare of a typhoon. A wave of electric sand exponentially fattening itself until taller than the tallest building. Coming in faster than a locomotive. If only this wave were Superman, but, instead, the wave was minor man playing his minor role in climate change. Baaquir put a bandana around his mouth. He closed his eyes. He pretended he would stay outside for the exfoliation but the wind came hard and he knew better than to be ridiculous. He went inside.

The dust storms did not used to be like this. Dust storms are for Sudan and the Arabian Penisula. Not the desert southwest. The housing boom of 2004 and 2005 and the subsequent bust meant that developers dug up land, and put houses into that dirt, but the plants and rocks and landscaping that usually follow didn't happen when no one bought the houses. Researchers speculate that the microorganisms that held down the soil trampled by bulldozer died and the soil became subject to wind.

Other researchers worry the giant dust storms carry microorganisms and pollutants unhealthy for your lungs. The blame always falls on the little guys.

Baaqir spent the next hour washing down his house. There was an inch of mud on the top of the pool. Phoenix charges a flat rate for water right now. He hosed down the rocks. The house looked forlorn covered in dust. He didn't want to live in a ghost town.

◎

Microbivalves

I knew oyster farmer who lived on the Puget Sound. He had so many oyster beds that he could barely see the ocean floor. Who needs the ocean floor when you have stacks of opaline shells tucking the whole fecund ocean between their halves? The oyster farmer offered me an oyster. No lemon. No mignonette. No Tabasco. The whole point of being an oyster farmer is that you don't need anything else. You can survive on the protein of oysters. The world could fall away and you would still have a house, a beach, a vocation, a dinner, and a moneymaker. Not everyone can grow oysters. Most people can't even open them. He is a gifted farmer. He knows how to seed the oysters directly in the sway of currents to bring the sweetest water, the most succulent plankton and algae passers-by. Oysters are the great filters of the ocean. The farmer does what he can to make sure the algae and the plankton swing by the beds abundantly or the oyster might turn to eating plastic and heavy metals and all the coffee Seattle runs down the storm drain and makes its way into the Puget Sound.

Palmed in the oyster farmer's hand, the oyster cinches shut. But he is a gifted farmer and a gifted metaphor-maker. He turns rock into sustenance. One knife jab and the hard shell turned to pulsing organ. Sexy oyster. All the genitals in one. Lick me, it seemed to say, so I did. The oyster tasted as shiny as the sun, which is why they grow in the sea in

Seattle—Seattleites like to keep the sun underground. Save it for a rainy day.

But this oyster was one of the last oysters, rain or shine. The farmer could not make a filter for the filters. The tides were turning red. The oyster industry was in collapse. As carbon dioxide warmed the skies, it also changed the chemical make-up of the ocean. The ocean went from Tang to limeade and there was not a mollusk in the world who preferred sour over sweet. Not a Kumomoto or a Sweetwater. Not a Hood Canal or a Fanny Bay. The names themselves suggested doughnut and apple pie, ice cream and caramel. You once put lemons on an oyster as a counterpoint. Now all you have is point point point, make a point. Blue point oysters. A redundancy. As redundant as the farmer who walks along the beach, stares out across the water, and sees the bottom of the vinegary, sexless ocean just fine.

◎

Biofuels Will Take You Home

I am traveling, by car, using regular old-fashioned gasoline, 140 miles from high-desert Flagstaff, Arizona, to low-desert Phoenix to visit Arizona State University's Biodesign Institute to learn how microorganisms can make fuel from the sun. Although the distance is not far, the territory you pass through is like traveling to nine different planets. Each zone hosts different dirt, flowers, animals, but all of them are sunny. In Arizona, the sun follows you everywhere. My friend calls Phoenix the Valley of the Shadow of Death for its pavement plan, its lack of water, its traffic, its sprawl, and for its heat. It is easy to be devout to this religion—hating Phoenix.

It is March on the roof the Environmental Engineering building and it's already hot. Regular July-in-the-rest-of-the-world type heat. There is still snow in Flagstaff, I keep reminding myself. The sun is everywhere, winking sinister "hello" up from the sidewalk, down from the sky, left from the parking structure, right from the glass building next door. I understand immediately why the work I've come to see happen, happens in Phoenix. Standing on a roof on the ASU campus at the end of winter and realizing I should have worn deodorant. I laugh that I brought my jacket at all, especially up here. But I can't take it off now because of the sweat stains. I am trapped under that flat blue sky of Arizona with my brown jacket which may as well be black as it absorbs the heat. I wonder what microorganisms are hatching in my armpits.

Hot, the roof is a natural place to think about two things—solar power and greenhouse gases, if not necessarily microorganisms. In Margaret Atwood's *Oryx and Crake*, people turn their air conditioners on in March, just like they do here in Phoenix. In her book, a whole planet turns Arizonan. From this roof, I can see pockets of palm trees transplanted from more formal deserts. Easy converts. Sand to sand. Dry to dry. From here, I can see mountains strangely shaped like meringue— their peaks are swept, but pointy and uneven, as if neither wind nor rain nor continental shift made them. They look like made-up and lopsided falling soufflés. It is a bad habit of mine, to want everything to be like food, as palatable as beer. Some people want mountains to be full of mineable ore. I want mine to be abundant, productive, edible. The mountains in Oregon are full of edible mushrooms. The rivers fatten with spawning salmon. You can even eat the ferns. The best I can think to do with a Phoenix mountain is to turn it into a metaphor of useful edibility.

Portland, Oregon starts with a P, as does Phoenix, but that's about all they have in common. They don't even have the "P" sound in common, just the letter. Portland is 2,000 miles away. Portland is green, mushrooms, water, salmon, coffee, and beer. Phoenix is brown, sand, Saguaro, golf, and sun. If left with Portland's list of plentiful offerings, you could survive forever. With the Phoenix list, you would most likely die.

There are naturally sustainable towns like Portland and unsustainable towns, and Phoenix might be the least sustainable of all. The best thing to do to Phoenix is to leave it, which I mostly try to do.

Recently, my husband Erik and I visited my old boyfriend Van in Portland. Van started his own beer brewing company. It rained the whole time we were there, that persistent we-live-inside-a-cloud rain that dampens your hair and leaves your socks wet. The kind that allows for beer and salmon and mushrooms and green. At his bar, a renovated gas station, we drank a glass of "Axes of Evil." Not as hoppy as the "Surly Overrated" or the boringly named "IPA." I pointed out the nice floors. Polished concrete. The cabinets. Remnants from the Portlandia building remodel. The counter tops. An old middle school gym floor. Portland never increases, never decreases. It maintains.

We talked about the difference between making things in Portland and making things in Phoenix. "Oh. We know a lot about water," I told Van. Van lives in Portland. I don't anymore. I'd rather live in Portland so I keep up on water news like I still live there. I pretend no knowledge about Phoenix sun.

"Phoenix has a TDS of 650. Portland's TDS is near zero. It's the softest water around. Soft as a baby's cheek." Van made his big smile which takes his face from thin and triangular to square and fully British.

I nodded. But I have no idea what TDS is. Apparently, I know nothing about water.

"TDS. Total dissolved solids." I thought about my bathroom shower. Lime. Calcium deposits. Who knows what else? I have used a chisel to a faucet in Flagstaff. But in Portland, mold grew on shower curtain doors. You couldn't get that off even with a chisel. Mold penetrates. You had to buy a new shower curtain—small things build up in all towns.

"Portland is the place to brew beer. You don't have to compensate for bad water." Erik, who listens to beer people better than I do, asked if Van filters his water like some breweries in Salt Lake City, where Erik and I lived before Flagstaff and where the total dissolved solids in the water are nearly as high as in Phoenix.

"We don't have to filter. The water is our baseline. Truly, for good beer, place only matters because that's where you get your water. Portland doesn't necessarily have the best brewers or the best equipment. Everywhere else you can get your hops flown to you. Your malt. But water. That's what makes your beer yours."

The water in Portland flows naturally from Mount Hood, Portland's very own mountain which makes Portland's very own beer. Water is to Portland as sun is to Phoenix—in most ways, too much. In Portland, treated water is released into the Willamette River, makes its way to the ocean where it's quickly fermented into clouds, which snow and rain down on Mt. Hood all over again. Portland recycles itself. You don't need to go anywhere.

In Phoenix, nearly everything comes from someplace else. The water is on loan from the Colorado which flows not anywhere nearby. Entire canals were built to force the water southward.

But one thing Phoenix does have in abundance is sun. A lot of sun without a lot of water is, in nature, not very useful. You can't grow avocadoes, oranges, or pecans without a lot of water. But when you're up on a rooftop in March in Phoenix and already ready for some air conditioning, the heat of the sun makes you think "abundance" in the same way nine months of every-day-rain in Portland makes you think of water's abundance. You don't like it. Too much of anything is never a good thing, so say the devout. At least with water, you can make beer. What can you do with all this sun?

Solar power. That is something you can do with all that sun. And one way to covert solar into power is through biofuel. Plants are already being used as biofuels like corn-based ethanol and soy/palm oil biodiesels. Corn, soy, and palm can be turned into fuel for your car, just like they can be used for fuel for your body (and, in the case of corn, sometimes in beer making). But growing food for oil has three problems: one, it is not scalable. You would have to cover all the arable land with corn, oil, and palm plants to use it to convert into energy for our cars. Feeding cars instead of people is ethically questionable. Second, it takes a lot of water per plant for the plant to grow into viable energy. And third, it takes a lot of energy to cook the plant into oil, cutting into purpose as well as profits.

But edible plants aren't the only organisms that harvest energy from the sun. Algae and cyanobacteria photosynthesize too. According to Rosa Krajmalnik Brown, a researcher at the Institute and Swette Center for Environmental Biotechnology, who also works on cataloging microorganisms that live in your stomach, cyanobacteria are much more amenable than algae.

"The genome of Synechocystis has been fully sequenced, and the microorganism provides a facile substrate for genetic modification of metabolic pathways to optimize yields of C-16 and C-18 lipids for biodiesel production," she says. Lipids. Microorganisms that produce lipids.

I am on the rooftop of a building looking at a model for what they hope will one day be a large-scale biofuel processing plant that converts lipids to biodiesel. Synechocystis, this tiny microorganism that is fast at work. It is like the cactus of microorganisms. It can survive crazy heat and even cold temperatures. Feed it a little CO_2 with a side of salt and nitrogen and it just gets fat. Stick some in a puddle at the end of a gas flue at a currently polluting power plant and it will turn that pollution into the same fuel that the power plant produces. Send some agricultural run-off laden with nitrogen and it will eat that up and turn it into more fat. These fatty lipids, these are fuel themselves. Put them in an oil tanker, send some to Portland where the only thing that doesn't grow so fast is sun.

Behold! Microorganisms that can turn solar power into fungible energies similar to oil. Fungibility is important. The ability to move fuel from place to place is almost as important as procuring the fuel itself. Getting the oil to where people need it the most, to heat and cool their homes, or, sometimes, so they can move their cars and their planes with movable fuel to take them where they want to go, is one of the reasons solar power has met so much resistance. Solar power in the form of fatty lipids can go anywhere using infrastructure that has been in place for years: refinery to tanker. Tanker to train. Train to tanker. Tanker to town.

I wanted to see this in person. Actually, I want to visit Van again and drink more Gigantic Beer in Portland but Portland is far and Phoenix is close and I am only so fungible. The Biodesign people seem to be amenable to people from Flagstaff trolling around their rooftops to see where all the sun goes.

Josh, a master's student in biophysics whose last name I neglect to ask for, who manages or grows or babysits the cyanobacteria (they are workers, plant-like photosynthesizers, tiny beings), works to explain green foam growing in open tubes stretched across the roof of the Chemistry building. He is very relaxed. He seems to have made friends with these microorganisms. Now, he sits back, talks about beer instead of microbes. Josh just received a beer-making kit from his girlfriend.

She regrets it because now that's all he talks about, making beer. Their living room is strewn with beer magazines, carboys, and different strains of hops. At least he's not talking only about cyanobacteria with his girlfriend, I joke. He looks at me blankly and says, "It's kind of the same thing. Yeast. Cyanobacteria."

I wonder if Josh is so laid back because he has all of these tiny organisms doing all this work for him. They're his. He might love them a little. More than he loved the algae. Josh just finished working with a team who was working with algae to harvest bioenergy. They ran into problems with the water—there wasn't enough of it (Arizona). In addition, by electrolyzing the water, unhealthy microorganisms grew, outnumbering the useful algae and preventing the algae from doing their photosynthetic lipid-making work.

The idea for both algae and photosynthesizing microorganisms is relatively simple: these photosynthesizing microorganisms use the sun as food, converting their extra energy into fatty lipids. The sun produces more food than the cyanobacteria can use. CO_2 and fixed nitrogen also feed the bacteria. The bacteria use that CO_2 and the sun, and a tiny bit of nitrogen as fertilizer, to produce fatty acid—lipids. What's so exciting is that this is not a biomass product that must then be processed, like corn. They can be directly harvested. The cyanobacteria act like little factories, producing tiny bits of fuel. The bacteria have done all the conversion inside themselves. Just like the forests, this fat is ready to burn.

It's like liposuctioning all the fat from all the fat Americans and filling your gas tank with it. You. Fungible. Human fat would need a lot more processing, and although there is plenty of fat in America, it's still not enough to last. We need something that likes to sit and expel fat all day long, every day, nonstop. These microorganisms seem to like their job here in Arizona. I wonder how long I would have to sit here for them to make me enough fuel to visit Van at his brewery where he could tell me more about the awesomeness of Portland beer.

Up here, on the roof, it doesn't look like you could get into much trouble with water. Long, flat, clear-plastic pipes were half-filled with water but the water is contained and it looks like less than a swimming pool's worth. Much less.

"We just had a plastic guy up here. He was trying to sell us some great plastic—the kind that UV rays don't turn brown. We brought him up here and showed him these." Josh points to a pile of discarded brown plastic pipes. "Those pipes? They're made of the same plastic he was trying to sell us. People understand sun but they don't understand Arizona sun. Brown's not good. Sun can't get through brown."

I ask why they didn't use glass. There is an advantage to being an English major, not a scientist. I can ask stupid questions.

"It's too expensive. It's breakable. It's heavy. But, if our tubes keep turning brown, maybe we'll try it."

It's then that I realize how early they are in the process. They're still buying and trying plastic from the "plastic guy." They're taking questions from English majors. They haven't ordered the plastic they'll need to cover acres of land. They'll probably have to invent the right kind themselves. The pipes I'm looking at, filled with microorganisms that make the water look blue-green, only run four across. It's the smaller of their two reactors, but the big one is not that big. The mechanism to harvest the fatty lipids hasn't even been attached to the extruding end. Even if it could, maybe they'd scrape off a barrel full of lipids. At full capacity, this reactor could produce about three barrels of oil-like substance a day. Not exactly enough to run the planet on.

Still, when I look through the semi-scuffed plastic, I can see little flecks riding on the blue-green waves.

"Those are the fatty lipids. Those things are the oil we're producing. Our own little Iran on the roof of the EE building."

They look like tiny bubbles but they aren't bubbles. Bubbles would have been a bad sign. Bad bubbles mean bad bacteria same as the problem with algae. It's hard to grow one thing and not grow another. Josh says it's always a fight—getting the cyanobacteria to grow while keeping other water- and sun-loving bacteria away. The best strategy was to keep the temperature a little colder than most bacteria liked. The cyanobacteria, unlike algae, don't mind it a little cold.

"Yeah, in July, we're running air-conditioning on our bacteria full-time."

It seems a little counterintuitive, running a power-grubbing machine to keep these little bio-machines running.

"Eventually, the microorganisms will create enough juice to run the air-conditioner themselves." I picture a person running on a treadmill to power a fan to keep themselves cool. Why not just sit and not move?

"Eventually, the system will be more sustainable. We'll use gray water and water from cement factories. We'll find ways to shade the plants when we move full-scale."

I like the confidence of when we move full-scale but right now the whole thing looks like little more than a chemistry experiment. Which I guess it is.

"What do they feel like? Those little flakes when you harvest them and put them in a barrel? Like a handful of dead cells?"

"No, no. We call them flakes and they do look flaky on the lip of the waves, but when you stick your hand it, it feels juicy—like sticking your hand in a vat of dishwashing liquid. It's liquid. Like oil."

I want to test this theory. I want to stick my hands deep into a vat of Dawn and pull out solar power. I want to dig deep and squeeze out a force that could catapult my car. I want to know what the excretion of tiny organisms could band together to produce and see it as a new kind of life. It was a new kind of life. Fatty lipids that work like oil that feels like Dawn dishwashing liquid that washes away the black oil stuck to the otter's coat. As if that otter swims in the ocean ever again. As if that egret flies again. There is something to metaphor here—if you can believe in conversion—in carrying one idea over to another, that's how you dig your way out of a pile of refuse, effluent, toxins, sorrow. You turn one idea into another without losing your scientist-eye of knowing the difference between the warmth made by methane gas and the warmth made by the sun.

The best thing, after climbing back through the door on the roof, is the air-conditioning. The other best thing is Josh offering us a beer from his fridge. The beer tastes okay—not too yeasty, not too hoppy. It doesn't have that buttery aftertaste like some home brews which indicates bacteria has infiltrated the system. It still has all the hallmarks of homebrew—a little too sour, a little too yeasty, and the total dissolved solids scratches my throat. Or at least makes me think perhaps better water would make this beer better.

So here's the plan. I will bottle up this fungible sun. Stick it in an oil tanker. I will send the sun now converted to flaky lipids up to Van in Portland. Van in Portland can use the flaky microbes to heat the water to sterilize his vats, barrels, and bottles. He can use the flaky lipids to power the machine that fills the bottles. Van can fill the sterilized bottles with Portland water converted into beer and send the beer back to me using fuel turned from the sun into fatty lipids to power the truck that drives the beer, converting what is mine in abundance into something that everyone can share.

Phoenix recycling sun for Portland. Portland recycling water for Phoenix. A way to maintain, even possibly sustain. And a way for me to learn to love Phoenix.

◎

Microbags

At Fry's Grocery and Drugstore, the plastic bags are tinted brown. Thin enough to see through, they should be strong enough to hold at least three items. But the clerks at Fry's dig their hands into the abundance of bags. Stacked like money, peeled like sawbucks, a bag wraps a carton of eggs. Another, a half-gallon of orange juice. Another, a pound of butter. Another, a quart of milk. A loaf of bread. You know the song. Each bag makes each item precious. How can I eat this butter now? I should preserve it in a cabinet of wonder but by the time I get home the cabinet of wonders becomes merely a refrigerator. The loaf of bread. The quart of milk. Each item reshelved in the icebox of my future—I now can make béchamel, French Toast, crème Anglaise, Pasta Carbonara, countries of recipes, thanks to bags of permanence and transportation.

The bags, emptied, do not realign. I cannot stack them. They do not fit in my billfold. I bunch them up. I crush them into the reusable canvas bags that I sometimes remember to take to the store. The bags live in the garage. Unlike the refrigerator, the garage is not airtight. Sometimes, I leave the garage door open. Sometimes, there is a wind. Sometimes the wind comes in and steals the plastic bags as if the wind had some groceries to make precious. The wind takes the bags, plasters them against Ponderosa, wraps them around pinecone, flags them against a decaying stick. The stick isn't going anywhere now. The Ponderosas preserved. The pinecones, seeding inside of the bag, with the benefit of a dusty rain, grow their own tree inside the bag. Inside the bag is a perfect microcosm. A hundred million tiny planets floating across the state, blowing their forevers across the highway, through the forests, across the ocean, establishing themselves as normal as continental cash.

◎

Microbiotics

Most of the time I'm kidding. The apocalypse. I'm not afraid. There's water in the pond on Butler Avenue. It is raining puffs of dust and wind. I have not seen an article about the bird flu all day. I have not even seen a bird. The Keystone Pipeline keeps a' comin', oil from sand—how can I worry we will ever run out of oil? I stock tomatoes— three Mason jars left. I have two packages of pork belly in the freezer. In bacon, we shall overcome? A pound of bonito flakes. May the ensuing apocalypse require miso soup! My munitions are no ammunition against any apocalyptic threat so I must not really be so worried.

And yet, on the top shelf, I keep an unused package of antibiotics. Azithromycin. A Z-pack my doctor gave me for a sinus infection I decided to make my immune system fight on its own to help stave off the antibiotic-resistant sinus infections of the future. The Z-pack is from 2011. It has probably expired. I wonder, at night, when I'm trying to fall asleep but not sleeping because of the bird, whether I should put the Z-pack in the freezer. I wonder if freezing the antibiotic would make it ineffective. I wonder why the doctors don't keep all the antibiotics in the freezer in case our apocalypse comes supplied with electricity. I wonder about apocalypses without electricity. I think about the cold whirl of wind, the dry pond, the car in the garage that is fully out of gas. I picture making the last batch of dashi broth to feed my son and my daughter. I picture spooning it in their mouths. Their heads are draped with washcloths to keep the fever down. They are bone-thin. They are wretched because the apocalypse courts Dickens. I think of my Z-pack. Will half an antibiotic work for each child? Is whatever bird flu they have contracted antibiotic resistant? Isn't the bird flu a virus anyway? Still, an infection. I do what I can. I will break each of the pills in half. I think *it's only six days, it's only six days, only six days*, and then everything will be better. The water will fill. The birds will return. The flu will subside. The car will learn to run on sand. We will make our way to the ocean where the bonito will leap into our arms, sacrificing themselves for our miso soup.

When I have these thoughts, I put my earplugs in, as if sealing off my ears can keep the thoughts out. But every once in a while, when even the earplugs don't work, I find myself creeping downstairs to the closet where I keep the azithromycin, next to a Ziploc of lost buttons and two hundred vials of albuterol solution that we could not nebulize into my daughter's lungs in an apocalypse that does not come endowed with electricity. I pray the apocalypse comes with electricity but I presume that is not the name for apocalypse at all. There are visions of the future that are too hard to see. I bring the box of antibiotics into my hand. I look at the expiration date. I think, that is not too long ago.

◎

Microapocalpyse

I only have one friend, Steve, who thinks we will survive the apocalypse. I stockpile jarred tomatoes. He stockpiles guns. We will need each other and will have to find a way to traverse the 500 miles that separates us. We will also need: sourdough starter made from wretched old grapes, fermenting in yet another Mason jar; one of those new-fangled straws that filters water even when you stick it into a nearly toxic cesspool; one cow or goat for milk; two chickens for eggs; a solar-powered automobile that can hold at least a family of four, a goat, and two chickens; sun; limes; avocado; salt. We will not need to reinvent the wheel or electricity. We may need to reinvent the Internet and flush toilets. We will need scissors, papers, pens, paperclips, staples—general office supplies—because if there is one thing we will surely miss, it is rebuilding the tax code. Benjamin Franklin said it was the library, or possibly fire stations, that made a civilization but if there is one thing that unites us all, it is our love of April 15th. Shared goals. A catholic expectation. We will need seeds from not-Monsanto and heart medication from not-Merck. We will need the old growth forest back. We will need the polar bear back. We will need that one frog who keeps changing his sex back and forth depending on how much Prozac is in the water to finally pick a team and stick with it. We will need an ocean full of fish and oysters who forgot the name red tide. We will need someone to make movies and someone to critique them. We may need books but possibly only ones that have nice things to say about fish. We will need to partner with the otters to learn how to stay warm in the winter and to discuss with the prairie dogs how to make a proper communal town where all the berries are good for all the dogs, prairie or not. We will need not only jarred tomatoes but lemon curd. We will need apple pie. We will need to learn to make béchamel with milk from our friend, the goat. We will need someone who knows how to make guitars and someone who knows how to play one. We will need a blanket, a square sewn by everyone who ever thought, man, this might be the end and then, wakes up the next day, happy that it isn't. In the end, we will need a lot of things but I think it's going to be OK because these days, Mason jars are plentiful and everyone I know is named Steve.

◎

Acknowlegments

5X5 –"Microsurgery"

Black Warrior Review – "Distracted Parents of the
    Micromanagement Era"

Essay Press – "Microwine"

Hotel Amerika – Microgalaxy & "Microwind" (as "Dear Galaxy" &
    "Dear Wind")

Menagerie – "Neutrinos"

Orion – "Microspikes" (as "House of Bees")

Sonora Review - "Bioefuels Will Take You Home"

Sweet – "Microencephaly"

Terrain.org – "Microapocalypse," Microbivalves," & "Microbiotics,"

The Account – "Microbags," "Microchip," "Microtrain,"
    & "Microsoccer "

The Collagist – "Microhematocrit" & "Microhabitat"

The Journal of Microliterature – "Microblogs"

The Normal School – "Micropreemies" & "Microorganisms"
    (as "Where the Tiny Things Are")

Wacawaw – "Microclimates, Lower Sonoran"

A number of these essays also appeared in the chapbook *Micrograms*,
    New Michigan Press, 2016.

◎

I want to thank Julie Paegle who read each of these tiny essays and this big one as well and for believing in the work and the idea behind the work. Thank you to Ander Monson, for his unending belief in me and for publishing some of the tiny issues in a tiny book, and thanks to Angie Hansen for championing the words and the work at work and Karen Renner for writing with me and making the books better, every week we meet to write. Thanks to Rebecca Campbell and Todd Grossman for sharing their love and their kids with me. Thanks to Steve Fellner for convincing me most of the time, the work is worth it. Thanks to Margot Singer for writing and editing with me and Lynn Kilpatrick for her sharing her big literary citizenship with me. I want to thank Eric Glomski of Page Springs Winery and Dr. Rolf Halden, Dr. Bruce Rittman, and Dr. Rosa Krajmalnik-Brown of Arizona State University's Biodesign Institute for their deep knowledge and willingness to share it with me. Thank you professors Katharine Coles, Donald Revell, Melanie Rae Thon, Karen Brennan, Jackie Osherow, and Robin Hemley for showing me how to focus on the most micro of things and how to explode them. I want to thank my colleagues, Lawrence Lenhart, Ann Cummins, Jane Armstrong, Erin Stalcup, and Justin Bigos for making our MFA program a great one. Thanks to Eileen Joy for taking this book on and to Valerie Vogrin for her incredible gifted editing skills and to both of them for their belief that paying attention to the tiny thing can make big things happen. These microessays have been lit-magged and chapbooked and have found their forever home in bound copies with Peanut books and I am grateful they will live openly and on-demandedly. Thank you immensely and especially, Gabriel Brandt for helping with the chemistry and with the details, both large and small. Everyone should have a reader, a chemist, and a friend like Gabe. Thank you always to Paige and Val and Mom whose brains and spirits suffuse every word I write and to Zoe and Max for loving me even though I spend too much time on my computer and to Erik who makes every word count and reads every one of them.

◎

Nicole Walker is the author of the forthcoming book *Sustainability: A Love Story*. Her previous books include *Egg, Micrograms, Quench Your Thirst with Salt,* and *This Noisy Egg*. She also edited *Bending Genre* with Margot Singer. She's nonfiction editor at *Diagram* and Associate Professor at Northern Arizona University in Flagstaff where it rains like the Pacific Northwest, but only in July.

Made in the USA
Middletown, DE
31 August 2018